T0340333

Coastal Asia, including Bangladesh and Indonesia, is one of the most vulnerable regions facing the impacts of climate change. A number of chapters in this book focus on the problems and solutions in this region, providing valuable, well-researched insights on natural resource governance and management that will support achieving the targets for SDG 14 and SDG 15.

> – **Marion Glaser,** *Work Group Leader, Social-Ecological Systems Analysis Group, Leibniz Center for Tropical Marine Research (ZMT), Germany*

. . . very relevant and timely publication on action based research that will help fill the gaps in gathering evidence to measure Bangladesh's progress for fulfilling the sustainable development goals. Rich in case studies from different parts of Bangladesh, this book is relevant for students, academics and practitioners who are learning about, as well as working on, the targets of the United Nations Sustainable Development Goals Agenda 2030.

> – **Saleemul Huq,** *Bangladesh Director, International Centre for Climate Change and Development (ICCCAD) and Senior Fellow, Climate Change, International Institute for Environment and Development (IIED), Bangladesh*

The issue of environmental sustainability is very important for Bangladesh since we are on the path to be recognized as a developing country. I believe the research findings of this book will be of great use to the scientific community, academics, professionals, practitioners, local government bodies and particularly to policy-makers to formulate long-term policies and strategies in addressing environmental sustainability in Bangladesh.

> – **Abdullah Al Islam Jakob,** *Deputy Minister, Ministry of Environment and Forests (Moef), Government of The People's Republic of Bangladesh*

Having the experience to educate students and young researchers from Bangladesh, I came to deeply know about the serious environmental issues affecting the country. The initiatives and ideas exposed in the present book are of crucial importance to inspire governmental authorities, policymakers and citizens of Bangladesh to be included in Sustainable Development Goals.

> – **Beatriz E. Casareto,** *Professor, Research Institute of Green Science and Technology and Graduate School of Science and Technology, Shizuoka University, Japan*

Addressing the concerns of environmental sustainability remains one of the major delivery challenges of the 2030 Agenda. The scholarly contributions contained in the volume, with impressive conceptual clarity and analytical depth, expose these challenges in the context of a dynamic developing country. These contributions will definitely enlighten efforts to embed dimensions of environmental sustainability in policies relating to inclusive growth and social cohesion.

> – **Debapriya Bhattacharya,** *Chair, Southern Voice Network of Think Tanks and Distinguished Fellow, Centre for Policy Dialogue (CPD), Bangladesh*

The Environmental Sustainable Development Goals in Bangladesh

This book examines the key Sustainable Development Goals (SGDs) relating to environmental sustainability and provides a cutting-edge assessment of current progress with the view of achieving these goals by 2030.

Within South Asia, the book pays particular attention to Bangladesh, as a country representative of emerging economies which are struggling to meet their goals. Drawing on the three pillars of sustainability, the volume addresses the following goals: Clean Water and Sanitation, Affordable and Clean Energy, Responsible Consumption and Production, Climate Action, Life Below Water and Life on Land (Goals 6, 7, 12, 13, 14 and 15). The book examines where progress has been made and why some key targets have not been achieved or will be difficult to achieve. The chapters focus on environmental sustainability in different sectors such as agriculture, renewable energy, fisheries and aquaculture and natural resource management.

The aim of this volume is to highlight key lessons and recommendations on how research in the various sectors can feed into the pathway of meeting the SDGs highlighted in this book. The analysis derived from Bangladesh can be used as a reference point for other developing nations in Asia, and globally, with a view to guiding policy for the achievement of the SGDs.

This book will be of great interest to students and scholars of sustainable development and climate change, as well as practitioners and policymakers involved in sustainable development and disaster management.

Samiya Ahmed Selim is Associate Professor and Director of Centre for Sustainable Development (CSD), University of Liberal Arts, Bangladesh.

Shantanu Kumar Saha is Assistant Professor at the Center for Sustainable Development, University of Liberal Arts, Bangladesh.

Rumana Sultana is Assistant Professor at the Center for Sustainable Development, University of Liberal Arts, Bangladesh.

Carolyn Roberts is the Frank Jackson Professor of the Environment at Gresham College, UK, as well as a Senior Scientist at the UK Knowledge Transfer Network (KTN) and Entrepreneur-in-Residence at Keele University, UK.

Routledge Focus on Environment and Sustainability

The Application of Science in Environmental Impact Assessment
Aaron Mackinnon, Peter Duinker and Tony Walker

Jainism and Environmental Philosophy
Karma and the Web of Life
Aidan Rankin

Social Sustainability, Climate Resilience and Community-Based Urban Development
What About the People?
Cathy Baldwin and Robin King

South Africa's Energy Transition
A Roadmap to a Decarbonised, Low-cost and Job-rich Future
Terence Creamer and Tobias Bischof-Niemz

The Environmental Sustainable Development Goals in Bangladesh
Edited by Samiya Ahmed Selim, Shantanu Kumar Saha, Rumana Sultana and Carolyn Roberts

For more information about this series, please visit: www.routledge.com/ Routledge-Focus-on-Environment-and-Sustainability/book-series/RFES

The Environmental Sustainable Development Goals in Bangladesh

**Edited by Samiya Ahmed Selim,
Shantanu Kumar Saha,
Rumana Sultana and
Carolyn Roberts**

LONDON AND NEW YORK

First published 2019 by Routledge

2 Park Square, Milton Park, Abingdon, Oxfordshire OX14 4RN

52 Vanderbilt Avenue, New York, NY 10017

Routledge is an imprint of the Taylor & Francis Group, an informa business

First issued in paperback 2020

British Library Cataloguing-in-Publication Data
A catalogue record for this book is available from the British Library

Library of Congress Cataloging-in-Publication Data
A catalog record for this book has been requested

ISBN: 978-1-138-61513-7 (hbk)
ISBN: 978-0-367-50768-8 (pbk)

Typeset in Times New Roman
by Apex CoVantage, LLC

Contents

Figures

Tables

About the editors

Carolyn Roberts

Professor Carolyn Roberts is the first Frank Jackson Professor of the Environment at Gresham College, delivering a series of public lectures in London, and online, on a wide range of environmental themes. She also works as a water and environment consultant, having undertaken innovative work in environmental science, management and technology for over thirty years.

Professor Roberts was formerly Director of the Environmental Sustainability Knowledge Transfer Network at the University of Oxford, her team funded by Innovate UK to link businesses and universities nationally. Her research at Oxford concerned engagement between the science community and local authorities on flooding. She still works as a technical assessor for Innovate UK grant applications. Previously she was Co-Director of the Centre for Active Learning (CeAL), one of the UK's national Centres for Excellence in Teaching and Learning, at the University of Gloucestershire, and Head of the School of Environment.

In addition to innumerable academic papers, Professor Roberts has authored, joint authored and edited four books with broadly pedagogic themes. She has spoken around the world on water management and sustainability-related projects undertaken in the UK, Europe, North and sub-Saharan Africa and Bangladesh, and increasingly on the issues and challenges of science communication. She was national Chair of the Society for the Environment, is a Vice President of the Institution of Environmental Sciences and a Trustee of the Worshipful Company of Water Conservators and was formerly Chair of the Higher Education Academy's Geography, Earth and Environmental Sciences Subject Centre Advisory Board.

Shantanu Kumar Saha

Dr. Shantanu Kumar Saha is an Assistant Professor at the Center for Sustainable Development, University of Liberal Arts Bangladesh. Academically he possesses a diverse and multidisciplinary background. He earned his PhD and master's degree from the College of Asia Pacific Studies (Social Science), Ritsumeikan Asia Pacific University, Japan. His graduate course work has covered a wide range of topics in the field of environment and development studies. Further, the concentration of his master's programme was in environmental policy and administration.

Dr. Shantanu has experience working in a cross-cultural environment. Throughout the seven years of his postgraduate study, he simultaneously worked as a teaching assistant for both undergraduate and graduate level courses at the Ritsumeikan Asia Pacific University, Japan. Additionally, he assisted professors in different research activities in the fields of environmental sciences, rural sociology and community capacity development.

Dr. Shantanu has received several scholarships and research grants throughout his academic career. He is familiar with both qualitative and quantitative research methodology as well as data analysis. His research interests include issues related to society, development and the environment. He is currently engaged in research on rural coping strategies in developing countries affected by extreme weather events, and is interested in pursuing further research in the field of climate change and sustainable development.

Samiya Selim

Dr. Samiya Selim is an associate professor and the director of the Center for Sustainable Development, University of Liberal Arts Bangladesh. Her specializations are in the areas of ecosystem-based management, sustainable livelihoods, socio-ecological systems, climate change adaptation and resilience and science-policy interphase. Currently her work is focused on ecosystem-based adaptation and integrated aquaculture in coastal areas of Bangladesh facing increased salinity and erosion.

Dr. Selim has two master's degrees in sustainable development and conservation biology from the University of Leeds and a PhD in marine ecology from the Animal and Plant Sciences Department, University of Sheffield, United Kingdom. She also has 10 years' working experience in research, project management and policy advocacy in the NGO sector in Bangladesh and the UK. She has been engaged in collaborative interdisciplinary research projects and consultancies with DFID, SEI, UNICEF, BRAC UK and USAID and has several publications in peer-reviewed journals.

Currently she is a member of the Integrated Marine Biosphere Research (IMBeR) Human Dimensions Working Group (HDWG), which focuses on the interactions between human and ocean systems and its goal is to promote an understanding of the multiple feedbacks between human and ocean systems.

Rumana Sultana

Dr. Rumana Sultana is an assistant professor in the Center for Sustainable Development, University of Liberal Arts Bangladesh. She has completed her PhD in environment and energy systems from Shizuoka University, Japan. Prior to her doctoral study, she completed her MS and BSc (honors) in geography and environmental studies from Rajshahi University, Bangladesh. She is a gold medalist of Rajshahi University for achieving outstanding results in her department and Faculty of Life and Earth Science. Her specializations are in the areas of climate change adaptation and resilience.

From 2013 to 2016, Dr. Sultana worked on the "Coral reef science for symbiosis and coexistence of humans and ecosystems under combined stresses" project for the Ministry of Education, Culture, Sports, Science and Technology, Japan, and the Global Coral Reef Conservation Project for the Mitsubishi Corporation, Japan. She has experience working on islands of the Pacific Ocean (Okinawa, Japan and Ishigaki Island, Japan), Indian Ocean (Albion, Mauritius) and Andaman Sea (Phuket, Thailand).

Dr. Sultana conducted extensive research, offered training on disaster risk reduction in the Gangetic islands to achieve sustainable households across rural Bangladesh. She has published several articles in internationally and nationally renowned journals. Currently she is a member of Japanese Coral Reef Society (JCRS) and Scientific Society of Advanced Research and Social Change, India.

Contributors

Sharmin Aftab
Current PGDEd Student
Institute of Education and Research (IER)
Khulna University, Khulna
Bangladesh

Md. Ali Akber
Assistant Professor
Environmental Science Discipline
Khulna University, Khulna
Bangladesh

Md. Shafiul Alam
Associate Professor
Department of Geography and Environmental Studies
University of Rajshahi
Bangladesh

Joy Bhowmik
Lecturer
Center for Sustainable Development
University of Liberal Arts Bangladesh (ULAB), Dhaka
Bangladesh

Shamik Chakraborty
JSPS-UNU Postdoctoral Fellow
Institute for the Advanced Study of Sustainability
United Nations University
Tokyo, Japan

Priyanka Chowdhury
Economic Research Officer
Department of Foreign Affairs and Trade
Australian High Commission, Dhaka
Bangladesh

Navojit Dastidar
Undergraduate Student
Department of Economics
North South University, Dhaka
Bangladesh

Rajan Chandra Ghosh
Lecturer
Department of Emergency Management
Faculty of Disaster Management
Patuakhali Science and Technology University, Dumki
Bangladesh

Md. Atikul Islam
Professor
Environmental Science Discipline
Khulna University, Khulna
Bangladesh

Shafiqul Islam
Assistant Professor
Center for Sustainable Development
University of Liberal Arts Bangladesh, Dhaka
Bangladesh

Zainu Sadia Islam
Completed MEng at University of Calgary, Alberta, Canada
Bangladesh

Sajid Iqbal
Founder
CHANGE
Dhaka
Bangladesh

Md. Jakariya
Professor
Department of Environmental Science and Management
North South University, Dhaka
Bangladesh

Andrew Jenkins
Fellow (Visiting) Judge Business School
University of Cambridge
England

Kazi Humayun Kabir
Assistant Professor
Development Studies Discipline
Khulna University, Khulna
Bangladesh

Nazmul Ahsan Khan
Professor
Department of Environmental Sciences and Management
North South University
Bashundhara, Dhaka
Bangladesh

Md. Wahidur Rahman Khan
MSc Student
Environmental Science Discipline
Khulna University, Khulna
Bangladesh

Sharmi Palit
Centre for the Study of Social Systems
Jawaharlal Nehru University, New Delhi
India

Md. Munsur Rahman
Professor
Institute of Water and Flood Management
Bangladesh University of Engineering and Technology, Dhaka
Bangladesh

Mohammad Rezaur Rahman
Professor
Institute of Water and Flood Management
Bangladesh University of Engineering and Technology, Dhaka
Bangladesh

Md. Rasheduzzaman
Former MS student
Department of Emergency Management
Faculty of Disaster Management
Patuakhali Science and Technology University, Dumki
Bangladesh

Carolyn Roberts
Professor of Environment
Gresham College, London
United Kingdom

Shantanu Kumar Saha
Assistant Professor
Center for Sustainable Development
University of Liberal Arts Bangladesh, Dhaka
Bangladesh

Samiya Ahmed Selim
Associate Professor
Center for Sustainable Development
University of Liberal Arts Bangladesh, Dhaka
Bangladesh

Md. Shamsuzzoha
Associate Professor
Department of Emergency Management
Faculty of Disaster Management
Patuakhali Science and Technology University, Dumki
Bangladesh

Mohammad Sujauddin
Assistant Professor
Department of Environmental Science and Management
North South University, Dhaka
Bangladesh

Rumana Sultana
Assistant Professor
Center for Sustainable Development
University of Liberal Arts Bangladesh, Dhaka
Bangladesh

Sabrina Zaman
Graduate student
Department of Environmental Sciences and Management
North South University
Bashundhara, Dhaka
Bangladesh

Foreword

In the trajectory of the world's development, economic development has been the highest priority since the industrial revolution. However, due to the uncontrolled desire to acquire more wealth in this capitalist society, few issues remained ignored and the world started facing different environmental and social problems in new waves. To address these issues global leaders decided to develop global sustainable development goals (SDGs) at the Rio+20 United Nations Conference.

It is believed that the SDGs are a roadmap to the future we want, since they reflect the need to incorporate social development alongside economic growth, while also considering environmental protection. Several nations' governments have begun to incorporate sustainable development in their planning and policy, and significant progress has been made in the last 20 years. We are starting to see progress because 193 countries in the UN have started working together to tackle the key development challenges around the world and progress towards a sustainable pathway.

Though the world has made good progress, the achievements have been uneven across countries. Some developing countries, particularly in Africa and South Asia, have made progress, but others are still struggling to achieve these goals. In the context of South Asia, Bangladesh is an emerging economy but lagging behind many countries in attaining certain goals. Bangladesh was ranked 120 out of 157 countries in the SDG Index and Dashboards Report 2017 by the UN Sustainable Development Solutions Network. According to the progress report on UN Sustainable Development Goals (SDGs), Bangladesh received red ratings on very few SDGs and yellow ratings for other SDGs, which actually indicates certain progress but also the need for significant work to overcome major challenges to meet the goals. Therefore, Bangladesh can be a good example to explore the challenges in-depth and measure how progress is being achieved. The issues faced in Bangladesh could also be a learning example for other developing countries, in particular for South Asian countries.

This book is intended to stimulate a dialogue on environmental sustainability and provides evidence for how Bangladesh is fulfiling the environmental sustainable development goals. Discussion and analysis from the selected action-based case studies show that the successful achievement of the environmental goals and targets could be built on support from society and scientific consensus. On the other hand, the research articles of this book, which cover different problems and solutions found in Bangladesh, are an important reference for exploring more on the progress so far and gaps remaining on achieving the environmental SDGs in a South Asian context. Further, other developing countries can also learn from the cases discussed in this book, to inform their policy framework. I hope this book will be a part of the great knowledge generation of the Sustainable Development Goals initiative.

Professor A. Veeramani, PhD
Professor Emeritus
College of Asia Pacific Studies
Ritsumeikan Asia Pacific University, Japan

Acknowledgements

This book is the end product of the collective efforts and hard work of several individuals who participated as well as contributed to the 2nd Annual Conference on Sustainable Development 2017 organized by Center for Sustainable Development, University of Liberal Arts Bangladesh. This conference provided a unique opportunity to bring together stakeholders from government, academia, private companies, international agencies, NGOs, and grassroots organizations to share practical solutions towards the achievement of the United Nations Sustainable Development Goals. The final outcome of the conference is this book, a collection of important research papers presented at the conference, on environmental sustainable development goals in Bangladesh.

First and foremost, we would like to thank the Conference Advisory Board Members whose guidance and support helped us to make the conference a success. We want to thank all the participants who presented their research work, to all the volunteers and staff at the conference, and to the group of participants who have continued to work with us on getting their papers ready for this book. We specially want to thank Professor Carolyn Roberts and Professor A. Veeramani for their additional time and effort in getting this book collection ready to be published.

Special thanks to Dr. Debapriya Bhattacharya and Dr. Saleemul Huq, both leading figures in the forefront of work around Sustainable Development and Climate Change in Bangladesh, who continue to support us as we all collectively work on this agenda in achieving SDG targets in Bangladesh.

We are sincerely indebted to our Vice Chancellor Professor Jahirul Huq and Professor Imran Rahman, Special Advisor to the Board of Trustees, University of Liberal Arts Bangladesh for their continuous support, time and encouragement during the conference, as well as for providing such an enabling environment at ULAB during the preparation of this book. Special thanks to our CSD dedicated team members, who have worked around the clock especially to Asif Bayezid and Mahdia Mehnaz Twinkle for their hard work in the backend preparation of the book. Thanks to Shafiqul Islam and Joy Bhowmik, our CSD faculties, for their enormous support in editing the book as well as for contributing individual chapters for this book.

Last but not least, we would like to express our sincere appreciation to the Government of Bangladesh for taking such strong measures in working towards the United Nations Sustainable Development Goals and we hope our work on academic research around the goals related to environmental sustainability can contribute towards achieving these goals.

Abbreviations

AIDS	Acquired Immune Deficiency Syndrome
BBS	Bangladesh Bureau of Statistics
BCSA	Bangladesh Cold Storage Association
BMD	Bangladesh Meteorological Department
BNHOC	Bangladesh Navy Hydrographic and Oceanographic Centre
BPDB	Bangladesh Power Development Board
BRAC	Bangladesh Rehabilitation Assistance Committee
CARIAA	Collaborative Adaptation Research Initiative in Africa and Asia
CEGIS	Centre for Environmental and Geographic Information Services
CES	Cultural Ecosystem Services
CIP	International Potato Center
CO_2	Carbon Dioxide
CS	Coefficient of Sensitivity
CSA	Cold Storage Association
CSD	Centre for Sustainable Development
CSFSN	Citizen Science Fishermen Safety Network
Cyn	Canyon
DANIDA	Danish International Development Agency
DFID	Department for International Development
DLRS	Directorate of Land Records and Surveys
DPHE	Department of Public Health Engineering
DT	Deep Tube Well
ECA	Ecologically Critical Area
ECOFISH-BD	Enhanced Coastal Fisheries in Bangladesh
ESV	Ecosystem Value
FAO	Food and Agricultural Organization
FGD	Focus Group Discussion

GAMs	Generalized Additive Models
GCRI	Global Climate Risk Index
GIEWS	Global Information and Early Warning System
GoB	Government of Bangladesh
GPS	Global Positioning System
GRAP	Graded Response Action Plan
GSB	Geological Survey of Bangladesh
HIV	Human Immunodeficiency Virus
ICDDR,B	International Centre for Diarrhea Disease Research, Bangladesh
ICZM	Integrated Coastal Zone Management
IDCOL	Infrastructure Development Company Ltd.
IDIs	In-Depth Interviews
IDRC	International Development Research Centre
IEA	International Energy Agency
IIED	International Institute for Environment and Development
IPCC	Intergovernmental Panel on Climate Change
IUCN	International Union for the Conservation of Nature
IWM	Institute of Water Modeling
JICA	Japan International Cooperation Agency
JNU	Jawaharlal Nehru University
KIIs	Key Informant Interviews
LCOE	Levelized Cost of Electricity
LGED	Local Government Engineering Department
LNG	Liquefied Natural Gas
MA	Millennium Ecosystem Assessment
MDGs	Millennium Development Goals
MMCF	Million Cubic Feet
MoEF	Ministry of Environment and Forestry
MoL	Ministry of Land
MPC	Mapping Science Committee
MSDI	Marine Spatial Data Infrastructure
MSL	Mean Sea Level
MW	Mega Watt
NE	North East
NGO	Non-Governmental Organization
NISE	National Institute of Solar Energy
NOAA	National Oceanic and Atmospheric Administration
NPV	Net Present Value
NRC	National Research Council
NSDI	National Spatial Data Infrastructure
NSDS	National Sustainable Development Strategy

OARE	Online Access to Research in the Environment
PM	Particulate Matter
PSF	Pond Sand Filter
PV	Present Value
PV-RO	Photo-Voltaic Powered Reverse Osmosis
RajuK	Rajdhani Unnayan Kartripakkha
RO	Reverse Osmosis
RWH	Rain Water Harvesting
SBL	Solar Bottle Lights
SDG	Sustainable Development Goal
SDI	Spatial Data Infrastructure
SDT	Shallow Depth Tube Well
SE	South East
SES	School of Environmental Sciences
SES	Social Ecological System
SHS	Solar Home System
SOB	Survey of Bangladesh
SoNG	Swatch-of-No-Ground
SPARRSO	Space Research and Remote Sensing Organization
SPI	Standardized Precipitation Index
SRE	Sustainable Rural Energy
SRL	Sea Level Rise
SST	Sea Surface Temperature
SWMC	Surface Water Modeling Centre
TDS	Total Dissolved Solids
TEK	Traditional Ecological Knowledge
TERI	The Energy and Resource Institute
ULAB	University of Liberal Arts Bangladesh
UNDP	United Nations Development Programme
UNEP	United Nations Environment Programme
UNESCO	United Nations Educational, Scientific and Cultural Organization
UNGA	United Nations General Assembly
USAID	United States Agency for International Development
USD	United States Dollar
VC	Valuation Coefficient
WB	World Bank
WCS	The Wildlife Conservation Society
WHO	World Health Organization

Introduction

Joy Bhowmik, Shantanu Kumar Saha
and Carolyn Roberts

Allegedly, the concept of 'sustainability' was originally coined by foresters, where it suggested only harvesting the amount of timber that a forest would yield in new growth (Wiersum, 1995). *Nachhaltigkeit* (the German term for sustainability), with its implication of 'balance' in using biological or environmental resources, was first used as long ago as 1713 (Wilderer, 2007), but the term gathered momentum in the later twentieth century when it referred to the maintenance of enduring systems and processes of all types, including those of human society. Much later, the term 'sustainable development', referring to the process of society moving closer towards sustainability, appeared in the *World Conservation Strategy* drafted by the United Nations Environment Programme (UNEP) and the International Union for the Conservation of Nature (IUCN) in 1980. According to the well-known 'Brundtland Report',

> sustainable development is development that meets the needs of the present, without compromising the ability of future generations to meet their own needs,
> (World Commission on Environment and Development, 1987)

a statement that strengthened the focus on human welfare still further, in the context of intergenerational equity. The Report urged stewardship of the natural environment, not only because of its intrinsic value but in order to preserve resources for adults and children everywhere, including those living in areas of the world that were less developed economically.

Operationalizing this concept has proved challenging and controversial in the face of multiple pressures from a rapidly growing global population with justifiable aspirations for a higher quality of life. In an attempt to reduce the complexity, sustainable development is often described simply in terms of three interlinked dimensions: environmental, economic and social (Strange & Bayley, 2008), all of which need to be addressed concurrently.

This is embodied in the definition of sustainability adopted by the United Nations in its Agenda for Development (1997), which asserts that

> Development is a multidimensional undertaking to achieve a higher quality of life for all people. Economic development, social development and environmental protection are interdependent and mutually reinforcing components of sustainable development.

The concept of sustainable development has encouraged decision makers to be conscious of the functions and services the natural environment provides. This is because environmental damage, and the potential risk of future damage, have a significant negative impact on the total development of a country. In practical terms, the theory of 'environmental sustainability' suggested a planning process that allows human society to 'live within the limitations of the biophysical environment'. As long as countries continue to meet their citizens' expectations for responsible environmental and social practices, the credibility and reputation of the country in terms of environmental sustainability will also continue to increase (Eccles *et al.*, 2014).

Background of environmental sustainability

Environmental sustainability is a condition combining ecosystem integrity, carrying capacity and biodiversity. It is now recognized that pressures on the natural environment arise in diverse ways, the balance between them varying from place to place across the world. Generically, environmental sustainability requires maintaining the planet's natural capital as both a source of economic inputs and a sink for wastes (Daly, 1973; Pearce *et al.*, 1990a, 1990b). At the source site, the harvest rates of resources must be kept within regeneration rates, as recognized in early forest management. At the sink sites, waste emissions from domestic, agricultural or industrial production must be controlled so as to not exceed the capacity of the environment to assimilate them without impairment (Goodland, 1995). There is, however, plenty of evidence that neither the harvesting nor the waste disposal is currently in balance with the carrying capacity of natural systems, and that the necessary circularity of environmental systems is not being maintained. As the global population has grown towards 8 or 9 billion, the direct influence of people on biological and environmental systems has caused massive loss of animal and plant species; deforestation; pollution of air, water and soil; over-fishing; widespread contamination of the oceans with plastics; encroachment of buildings on river channels; loss of wetlands to agriculture and construction; over-exploitation of groundwater; and land degradation resulting from excessive use of chemical fertilizers and pesticides. These pressures are compounded by the gradual but seemingly inexorable shift in climate associated with anthropogenic releases of 'greenhouse gases' such as carbon dioxide and methane into the Earth's atmosphere, reaching levels far beyond those ever experienced during human occupancy of the planet. Deforestation, burning of fossil fuels and a mass of other human activities have raised average global surface temperatures and triggered instabilities in weather patterns, the presence of surface water, ice sheet margins and the strength of ocean currents. The world is becoming a less hospitable place for humanity, and the situation is clearly not sustainable, by any definition of the term.

The protection of natural systems represents not an overarching panacea for achieving economic vitality and social justice, but a necessary component of an entire system for achieving economic, social and environmental 'sustainability' in the longer term, in which economic reforms and social reforms are as important (Basiago, 1999). In 1987, this was represented by the formulation of the so-called 'Millennium Development Goals', ranging from commitments to halve extreme poverty rates, provide universal primary education, and halt the spread of HIV/AIDS, which at that time was ravaging populations in Africa and some other developing areas. The goals galvanized efforts, particularly to meet the needs of the world's poorest people.

The term 'Sustainable Development Goals' (SDGs) refers to a second agreement of the United Nations Conference on Sustainable Development. On September 25, 2015, the leaders of 193 countries unanimously adopted the post-2015 international development agenda for the period of 2015–2030. With 17 goals and 169 targets, the SDGs represent a bold new agenda to end poverty and remove its root causes, to fight inequality, to tackle the adverse effects of climate change and to ensure a sustainable future for all (United Nations, 2015). The agenda is inclusive and broader than the original agreement on the Millennium Development Goals. The SDGs are intended to guide national choices now and maintain progress towards genuine environmental sustainability, in order to improve citizens' future lives. Crucially, reciprocity amongst the SDGs is realized; success in one arena will improve the chances of success in others, and failure will promote failure. Dealing with the impacts of climate change, eradicating poverty through achieving gender equality and better health and fostering peace and inclusive societies will all reduce inequalities and help economies prosper (United Nations Development Programme, n.d.).

Moving Bangladesh from MDGs to SDGs

The world has undoubtedly witnessed significant progress towards achieving some of the MDGs. Global statistics have revealed that an estimated 130 million fewer people were living in extreme poverty in 2015 than in previous years. Child mortality rates fell from 103 deaths per 1,000 live births to 88, and life expectancy rose from 63 years to nearly 65. Another noteworthy achievement was that an additional 8% of the developing world population had access to clean water (UNDP, 2015); similarly there was gain in the provision of improved sanitation services, by some 15%. Unfortunately, such progress was not uniform.

Bangladesh, in comparison with some other developing countries, was a relatively strong performer in relation to the original Millennium Development Goals. The country's economic position has for some time been underpinned by export-oriented industrial activities such as textiles and ready-made clothing, leather goods, shipbuilding and shipbreaking and a cluster of agricultural products including fish, seafood and jute. Domestically, food processing, steel and a burgeoning information technology sector have been important, and offshore gas fields are still being explored and exploited. Bangladesh is also the beneficiary of financial remittances from the large number of Bangladeshi people working or permanently resident overseas, although these may be expected to diminish over time as migrants' connections with their native country weaken. Growth in the manufacturing sectors saw the country move from being one of the world's poorest to its current status as an emerging economy, and analysts agree that significant progress has been made in reducing the headcount of people in poverty, and in reducing the poverty gap ratio (more than 45% of the extremely poor have been pulled out of the poverty trap). Malnourishment and the number of underweight children under five years of age have both decreased, although neither has been eliminated. Health care is generally improving: infant mortality rates and the maternal mortality ratio have both dropped. The proportion of one-year-old children immunized against measles and polio has increased, and deaths from malaria and tuberculosis have fallen. Educationally, the net enrolment in primary schools has increased, and gender parity has almost been achieved in primary and secondary education, in both rural and urban areas. Access to high quality drinking water has also improved significantly (WHO, 2015).

Encouraged by these achievements in relation to the implementation of the Millennium Development Goals, Bangladesh has turned its attention to the post-2015 sustainable development agenda, explicitly adopting eleven of the most relevant Sustainable Development Goals, 58 targets and 241 measurable indicators, in its post-2016 development agenda. The new focus for 2030 is particularly on eradicating poverty and inequality, ensuring food security and adequate nutrition for all, particularly marginalized communities, and improving human resources potential through technical education and vocational training, Additionally, the country is emphasizing universal access to health and family planning services, and maintaining environmental sustainability through the creation of climate change-resilient infrastructure. This is an ambitious vision.

Bangladesh's preparedness for the SDGs journey

Vision must nevertheless be tempered by realism. Bangladesh has maintained an enviable average annual growth rate in gross domestic product (GDP) of about 6% for more than a decade, with the rate exceeding 6% in the three consecutive years to 2014 (World Bank, 2014), rising to over 7% in 2017. Population growth rates have fallen substantially, with the annual census for 2011 suggesting some 153 million people live within the borders, and a current growth rate of about 1.65% per annum; it seems that with the investment in education, people are reducing their intended family size. The sustained economic growth has hence improved average per capita income, and the country is closing on its target of becoming a middle-income economy by 2021. Bangladesh's emerging economy nonetheless remains vulnerable, and socio-economic progress has already been constrained by the availability of good quality agricultural land and water for the densely-packed rural population, the impacts of progressive climate change and other environmental limitations. Extreme flood events triggered by exceptionally strong monsoons, storm surges, sea level rise and associated coastal erosion and increasing drought frequency in the north and west of the country are adding to the reality of the pressures. Bangladesh lost an estimated 5.9% of GDP to storms from 1998–2009 (ICCCAD/IPCC, 2014) despite the counter-intuitive effect of increasing purchases of repair materials tending to raise GDP. To try to maintain its economic growth, Bangladesh published a National Sustainable Development Strategy (NSDS) in 2013, squarely to meet the challenges of economic, social and environmental sustainability; it also represents an effort by the Government to meet international obligations to the global sustainable development agenda.

The vision embodied in the NSDS was developed through extensive consultation with national and regional stakeholders, by focusing on the following aspiration:

> Achieving a happy, prosperous and enlightened Bangladesh which is free from hunger, poverty, inequality, illiteracy and corruption, and belongs completely to its citizens and maintains a healthy environment.
> (NSDS, 2013)

The Strategy was based on the political commitment of the Government of Bangladesh to a long-term development vision which mainstreamed sustainable development challenges across different sectors, and integrated economic, social and environmental objectives in the manner suggested in Agenda 21 of the Rio Deceleration, the Johannesburg Declaration, and the Ministerial Declaration of Implementation of Environment and Development in Asia and the Pacific. The NSDS incorporated the Sixth Five-Year Plan (FY2011–FY2015, now superseded by the Seventh Five-Year Plan FY2016–FY2020), the Perspective Plan of Bangladesh 2010–2021 and other pre-existing sectoral plans, policies and strategies. The Perspective Plan (2012) envisioned that by 2021 the war against poverty will have been won and the country will have crossed the 'middle income' threshold, with the basic needs of the population ensured and their basic rights respected. This will be a time when everyone is adequately fed, clothed and housed, and has access to health care, sustainably and without damaging the environment.

The NSDS actually had a long gestation period. The United Nations Environment Programme and the Government of Bangladesh came to an agreement in mid-2007 to prepare the NSDS for Bangladesh and to establish an institutional structure in the form of a National Commission on Sustainable Development. Consequently, Bangladesh's NSDS preparation was based on the United Nations Environment Programme's guidelines, which defined its principles, functions, role and elements, and the process for managing sustainable development policies and actions in the country. The preface to the NSDS noted the twin objectives:

> . . . of formulating strategies to meet the challenges of economic, social and environmental sustainability faced by the economy as well as meeting international obligation of our country to global sustainable development principles and agenda. Meeting the sustainable development challenges will need raising the awareness and understanding of people of the challenges and coordinated efforts at the local, regional, national and global levels.

The approaches and principles that followed for the formulation of the NSDS for Bangladesh emphasized the need for long-term vision, building on existing mechanisms, strategies, capacities and learnings, and high-level Government and lead institution commitment.

To fulfil the vision of sustainable development, five priority areas were identified:

- Sustained Economic Growth
- Development of Priority Sectors
- Urban Development

- Social Security and Protection
- Environment, Natural Resource and Disaster Management

and three cross-cutting issues which were important for all five strategic priority areas, namely:

- Disaster Risk Reduction and Climate Change
- Good Governance
- Gender

Despite the work in progress towards many of the MDG targets, major challenges remained for Bangladesh in 2013, especially with regard to the hunger-related indicators such as MDG-1 (eradicate extreme poverty and hunger), MDG-5 (improve maternal health) and MDG-7 (ensure environmental sustainability). Despite the development of national standards of scientific expertise, and some government action, the last of these appeared particularly unlikely to be met as natural resources were progressively diminished by industrial encroachment, pollution and the impact of climate shifts on agriculture. Considering the MDGs' limitations, the drafting and adoption of the new SDGs created an opportunity to refresh engagement with issues such as inequality, employment and inclusive growth, child nutrition, maternal health, education, governance, energy and the environment.

According to the SDG Index and Dashboards Report from the UN Sustainable Development Solutions Network, four years later Bangladesh was ranked 120 out of 157 countries, with an unfortunate 'red' rating on ten of the 17 SDGs, indicating that major challenges still need to be overcome to meet the goals (Sachs *et al.*, 2017). Bangladesh was not unusual but scored marginally lower than most South Asia countries – behind its near neighbours India, Myanmar and Thailand, but ahead of Pakistan. Notably, SDG 7: ensure access to affordable, reliable, sustainable and modern energy for all; SDG 9: industry, innovation and infrastructure; SDG 11: sustainable cities and communities; and SDG 14: conserve and sustainably use the oceans, seas and marine resources for sustainable development were amongst those Goals for which Bangladesh received 'red' ratings for lack of progress.

Bangladesh did receive 'yellow' ratings on three areas where significant progress is being made, particularly on SDG 1: tackling poverty, SDG 10: reduced inequality and SDG 13: climate action. Bangladesh performed well in some sectors, reducing the emission of carbon dioxide through investing in renewable energy and imported advanced technologies. Noteworthy, too, is the progress on clean water and sanitation: SDG 6 is awarded only an 'orange' status for the indicator currently, but with suggestions that the latest figures for freshwater withdrawal from renewable sources as well as groundwater depletion are promising. These 2017 indicators give a useful snapshot but do not allow direct year-on-year comparisons, as the composition of the metric has been adjusted since the previously published values.

Major challenges for environmental sustainability

Viable future development in Bangladesh depends on environmental sustainability, since continuity of human life requires a dynamic balance between human, social and economic systems and the ecological systems that provide ecosystem services (Norton & Haskell, 1992). The challenges to environmental sustainability in Bangladesh originate from both internal external factors. Internally, accelerating growth in agricultural output, faster growth in manufacturing industry and development of fossil fuels have been associated with degraded agro-ecosystems, groundwater depletion, damaged rivers, wetlands and coastal zones, deforestation and desertification. Deforestation in Bangladesh has increased at an alarming rate, which is not only generating carbon emissions but also causing soil erosion and land desertification (Wolf, 1988). Urban environments, especially for the sixteen million people living in the Greater Dhaka conurbation, are particularly poor. This is reflected in the 'red' indicator awarded to SDG 11, sustainable cities and communities (Sachs *et al.*, 2017); poor air quality, lack of access to healthy drinking water, high risk of flooding and absence of a reliable electricity supply affects both people's livelihoods and their quality of life.

Externally, the most critical sustainability concern for Bangladesh is human-induced climate change (IPCC Intergovernmental Panel on Climate Change, 2014; Brown & Young, 1990). It is now recognized internationally that although Bangladesh is at the forefront of adverse climate change impacts, these are generated largely from beyond its boundaries. ICCCAD/ IPCC (2014) have suggested that there could be a decrease of about 50% in the most favourable and high-yielding South Asian wheat area due to heat stress if CO_2 levels are doubled, as seems likely unless there is serious multinational intervention to reduce atmospheric greenhouse gases. Moreover, in terms of heat stress, current temperatures are already approaching critical levels during the susceptible stages for rice growth in Bangladesh between March and June. With hotter and wetter conditions, human health may also be compromised by increases in infectious diseases such as cholera, dengue and diarrhea. More frequent and severe floods, tropical cyclones, storm surges and droughts pose severe threats to growth and the achievement of the SDGs in Bangladesh, too; the population at risk of sea level rise is predicted to grow to 27 million by 2050, and seawater inundation threatens agriculture as well as people. Waterlogging and salinization lead to land degradation, which has serious adverse implications for food production (Postel, 1990). There is also a regional challenge to achieving sustainability; decline of discharge in trans-boundary rivers, in part a result of impoundments upstream, has resulted in river siltation and desertification in northwestern parts of the country (Salman & Uprety, 2002).

The interactions amongst different global and local challenges to sustainability are manifold and complex. It is well understood that the damaging effects of climate change are likely to fall hardest on those poorer countries least equipped to cope with the consequences, and where technological solutions are very distant. But locally the inequalities can be greater than that. For example, Bangladeshi women often are not taught to swim, and may sometimes risk death in the face of imminent flooding because they are reluctant to depart from their houses alone. Moreover, the ICCCAD/IPCC (2014) also suggests that gender-based violence can be an indirect social consequence of climate-related disasters and slow-onset climate events, as a result of stress, tension, loss and grief. These multifaceted interconnections are characteristic of genuinely 'wicked' problems (Rittel & Webber, 1973) that resist easy resolution.

About this book

Environmentally sound development calls for actions based on thorough research and analysis simultaneously to restore and maintain environmental health, while pursuing socio-economic development. This book highlights the range of interconnected problems and solutions related to environmental sustainability that are being explored and addressed in Bangladesh (research for one paper was undertaken in India, but the results are eminently transferable), focusing on sectors such as agriculture, renewable energy (solar and biogas), fisheries and aquaculture, diffusion and continuation of agricultural technology and natural resource management, but is also relevant to other developing South Asian countries. It is organized around examples from specific sustainable development goals that have a strong environmental focus: SDG 6: Clean Water and Sanitation, SDG 7: Affordable and Clean Energy, SDG 12: Sustainable Consumption and Production, SDG 13: Climate Action, SDG 14: Life below Water and SDG 15: Life on Land. Each part contains one or more case studies that provide readers with some insights into the nature of the sustainable development challenge, allow them to consider the current position and foster understanding of the progress towards a solution. The research process in Bangladesh is not always easy, and the book is unusual in being based largely on the work of Bangladeshi academics and policy-makers, often working in conjunction with local communities in an attempt to secure a better future for everyone.

Part 1: Sustainable Development Goal 6: clean water and sanitation

Bangladesh has experienced a series of crises in the provision of sufficient potable drinking water for its population, and to support their agriculture. The presence of arsenic in groundwater in the aquifers of the Ganges and Brahmaputra deltas is well known, and its health impacts have been the subject of much research. This chapter explores a potential response to the presence of salinity and microbial contamination of water in many rural coastal areas. Desalination is not a universally accepted solution except in cases of acute water shortage, since it often depends on fossil fuel-derived energy to drive the technology, and high levels of technical expertise. However, Bangladesh's high levels of solar insolation do appear to offer some potential to exploit links between solar power and drinking water production in rural communities threatened by saline intrusion.

Part 2: Sustainable Development Goal 7: affordable and clean energy

Some sustainable development technologies are very simple, and their implementation depends not so much on technical expertise or high levels of investment, but on their acceptability to potential user populations. Solar bottle 'lights' can immediately provide very cheap daytime lighting inside otherwise dark houses, including densely packed shanties. Householders can reduce energy bills, carbon footprints and the risk from illegal connections to mains electricity supplies, and small businesses and residents can function more effectively. However, solar bottle lights' very simplicity and cheapness may promote feelings of worthlessness amongst those who rely on them. This chapter describes the process of implementing an innovation that provides a temporary solution to a sustainable development challenge, whilst longer term energy solutions for poor people in large cities such as Dhaka are awaited.

Part 3: Sustainable Development Goal 12: ensure sustainable consumption and production

The case study introduced in Chapter 3 explores the economic and technical feasibility of solar-biomass hybrid cold storage. Agriculture is the highest contributing sector of Bangladesh's gross domestic product (GDP), and there is great potential to produce perishable vegetables if the challenges of installing and running cold storage can be met. The research evaluates the potential scope for implementing solar-biomass hybrid cold storage in rural areas where no grid connection is expected to be available for over a decade, but it also highlights the crucial requirement for a technically trained workforce.

Part 4: Sustainable Development Goal 13: climate action

This part of the book comprises four chapters that explore different types of response to climate change, and the action required to mitigate or respond to it. Chapter 4 is a sociological study that bridges the gap between societal understanding, awareness and governmental laws from the perspectives of young people experiencing air pollution. Although the research was undertaken in New Delhi, India, the results are clearly transferable to the contaminated environments of Dhaka and other major Bangladeshi cities.

Chapter 5 discusses the impacts of progressive sea level rise and cyclones on arable agriculture along the Bangladesh coast, focusing on the adaptation practices currently used by farmers to fight against these climatic stressors. Concluding, the authors emphasize the need for changes in adaptation techniques to raise the resilience of the farmers, recommending that government and non-government organizations collaborate with the coastal communities to strengthen the adaptation programmes.

Chapter 6 describes a piece of action research highlighting how northern Bangladeshi farmers cope with recurrent water shortages. This, and the following chapter contribute to achieving SDG target 13.1, which is to strengthen resilience and adaptive capacity to climate-related hazards and natural disasters. The chapter presents some useful adaptation measures that are currently practiced by farmers, such as changing crops and cultivation times, plowing the land in anticipation of drought, using composted manure to improve the physical properties of their soil and digging irrigation ponds to create water reservoirs. This chapter also discusses some alternative options to allow households to recover from the impacts of drought.

Finally, Chapter 7 addresses the same SDG target in the context of excessive flows of water, by exploring the cross-cutting strategies used by Padma River islanders to mitigate their damage and losses from floods. River and sea flooding is a major challenge to economic development in Bangladesh, and the physical location of the country means that massive flood engineering schemes would be of limited value; reliance will need to be placed on such community and household-level tactics.

Part 5: Sustainable Development Goal: 14: life below water, and Sustainable Development Goal 15: life on land

This part of the book comprises case studies looking at the management of water and land ecosystems, and their management, particularly in the unique area of the Sundarbans. Chapter 8 surfaces the need for the inclusion of cultural ecosystem services in conservation and management policies and practices for mangrove ecosystems, addressing both SDGs 14 and 15 in the unique World Heritage Site of the Sundarban mangrove forests.

Chapter 9 assesses the ecosystem service value of southwest coastal Bangladesh, in the same area. Quantification of the different ecosystem services can assist with sustainable management of natural resources, if the technological challenges of establishing accurate data can be overcome, perhaps using satellite imagery. The discussion suggests that special attention to the ecosystem functions of mangrove forests is necessary to balance the relationship between the livelihoods of local farmers and ecosystem services.

The last chapter argues that where many different stakeholders work within the same complex jurisdiction, effective Spatial Data Infrastructure development can yield sustainable development benefits. In this context, the chapter explores the opportunities and challenges associated with integrating Marine Spatial Data Infrastructure (MSDI) into management of the mangrove forests of Bangladesh.

Progress towards the SDGs will require strong and effective institutional mechanisms involving stakeholders from public and third sector organizations, governments and their agencies, businesses and the private sector, civil society, knowledge communities and development partners around the world. It is hoped that this book will form part of the great Sustainable Development Goal initiative to set out the vision for similar cases and for embedding sustainability in all aspects of operations, learning, research, engagement and governance.

References

Agenda for Development. (1997). New York, NY, USA: United Nations.

Basiago, A. D. (1999). Economic, social and environmental sustainability in development theory and urban planning practice. *The Environmentalist, 19*, 145–161.

Brown, L. R., & Young, J. E. (Eds.). (1990). Feeding the world in the nineties. In *State of the World, 1990*. New York: W. W. Norton & Company.

Daly, H. E. (Ed.). (1973). *Towards a Steady State Economy*. San Francisco: W. H. Freeman.

Eccles, R. G., Ioannou, I., & Serafeim, G. (2014). The impact of corporate sustainability on organizational processes and performance. *Management Science*, *60*(11), 2835–2857.

General Economics Division. (2012). *Perspective Plan of Bangladesh 2010–2021: Making Vision 2021 A Reality*. Dhaka: Planning Commission, Government of the People's Republic of Bangladesh.

General Economics Division. (2013). *National Sustainable Development Strategy (2010–2021)*. Dhaka: Planning Commission, Government of the People's Republic of Bangladesh.

Goodland, R. (1995). Environmental sustainability: Universal and non negotiable. *Ecological Applications*, *6*(4), 1002–1017.

ICCCAD/IPCC. (2014). *What Does the IPCC Say about Bangladesh?* ICCCAD Briefing, October. Retrieved from http://icccad.net/wp-content/uploads/2015/01/IPCC-Briefing-for-Bangladesh.pdf

Intergovernmental Panel on Climate Change. (2014). *Synthesis Report*. Contribution of Working Groups I, II and III to the Fifth Assessment Report of the IPCC [Core Writing Team, R. K. Pachauri & L. A. Meyer (Eds.)]. Geneva, Switzerland: IPCC, 151pp.

Norton, B. G., & Haskell, B. D. (Eds.). (1992). *Ecosystem Health: New Goals for Environmental Management*. Washington, DC: Island Press.

Pearce, D. W., Barbier, E., & Markandya, A. (Eds.). (1990a). *Sustainable Development: Economics and Environment in the Third World*. London: Edward Elgar Publishing Limited.

Pearce, D. W., Markyanda, A., & Barbier, A. (1990b). Blueprint for a green economy. *Ecological Economics*, *7*(1), 75–78.

Postel, S. (Ed.). (1990). Saving water for agriculture. In *State of the World, 1990*. New York: W. W. Norton & Company.

Rittel, H. W. J., & Webber, M. M. (1973). Dilemmas in a general theory of planning. *Policy Sciences*, *4*, 155–169.

Sachs, J., Schmidt-Traub, G., Kroll, C., Durand-Delacre, D., & Teksoz, K. (2017). *SDG Index and Dashboards Report 2017*. New York: Bertelsmann Stiftung and Sustainable Development Solutions Network (SDSN).

Salman, S. M. A., & Uprety, K. (2002). *Conflict and Cooperation on South Asia's International Rivers: A Legal Perspective*. Washington, DC: World Bank Group.

Strange, T., & Bayley, A. (2008). *Sustainable Development: Linking Economy, Society, Environment*. Organization for Economic Co-operation and Development (OECD): United Nations Population Division. World Population Prospects.

United Nations. (1997). *Agenda for Development*. New York, USA: UN.

United Nations. (2015). *Transforming our world: The 2030 Agenda for Sustainable Development*. United Nations. Retrieved from https://sustainabledevelopment.un.org/content/documents/21252030 Agenda for Sustainable Development web.pdf

United Nations Development Programme. (n.d.). Retrieved from www.undp.org/content/undp/en/home/sustainable-development-goals.html

United Nations Development Programme. (2015). *Human Development Report: Work for Human Development*. New York, USA: UNDP.

Wiersum, K. F. (1995). 200 years of sustainability in forestry: Lessons from history. *Springer-Verlag: Environmental Management, 19*, 321. https://doi.org/10.1007/BF02471975

Wilderer, P. A. (2007). Sustainable water resource management: The science behind the scene. *Integrated Research System for Sustainability Science, 2*, 1–4. DOI: 10.1007/s11625-007-0022-0

Wolf, E. C. (1988). Avoiding a mass extinction of species. In World Watch Institute (Ed.), *State of the World*. New York: W. W. Norton & Company.

World Bank. (2014). *World Development Indicators Database*. Washington, DC. Retrieved from http://data.worldbank.org/data-catalog/world-development-indicators/wdi-2014

World Commission on Environment and Development. (1987). *Our Common Future*. Oxford, UK and New York, NY, USA: Oxford University Press. Retrieved from www.un-documents.net/our-common-future.pdf

World Health Organization. (2015). *Global Health Observatory*. Retrieved from www.who.int/gho/en/

Part 1

Sustainable Development Goal 6

Clean water and sanitation

1 Drinking water supply through reverse osmosis technology

A solution for water shortages in coastal rural areas of Bangladesh

Md. Shamsuzzoha, Md. Rasheduzzaman and Rajan Chandra Ghosh

Introduction

Clean freshwater is an essential resource for drinking, cleaning and sanitation, and a suitable (adequate, safe and accessible) supply is fundamental to sustaining healthy life. Improving access to safe drinking water can result in tangible benefits to health (Wingender & Flemming, 2011), but sources need to be sustainable. Access to clean water has rapidly become a significant worldwide problem (Gleick, 1993). Currently, around 1.2 billion people globally do not have access to satisfactory clean water, and with present rates of population growth and the effects of climate change, the problem of access to clean water is expected to escalate (Alkhatib, 2013). Freshwater shortages and unreliable water quality are considered major hindrances to achieving sustainable development and improvement to the quality of people's lives (Shrimali, 2015). Hence in many parts of the world there is a need to explore, develop and manage alternative sources of safe drinking water (Cotruvo *et al.*, 2010), and Bangladesh is no exception. Achieving this aim would support progress towards United Nations Sustainable Development Goal 6 (safe water and sanitation).

Groundwater has traditionally been the main source of drinking water in much of coastal Bangladesh, as in other similar areas of the world, but in recent years this supply has been problematic because of lowering of the water table, arsenic contamination, saline intrusion from the sea and the non-availability of accessible aquifers (Islam & Ahmad, 2004). Because of the frequency of natural disasters, and damaging artificial alterations to formerly natural settings, groundwater supplies are becoming more vulnerable day by day (Basar, 2012; Khanom & Salehin, 2012). Consequently, lack of access to safe drinking water has been identified as one of the critical issues in the daily life of these coastal households.

Desalination using reverse osmosis (RO) is potentially a solution for regions where fresh drinking water is under threat. Reverse osmosis is a membrane-based process technology which purifies water by separating out the dissolved material, controlling acidity and removing any bacterial contamination from feed streams (Garud *et al.*, 2011). If power is available and the equipment can be maintained properly, it is a source of water that does not diminish during times of drought or other natural calamities, thus helping to ensure adequate pure water supplies throughout the year. Cheah (2004) described an energy-efficient, cost-competitive, small-scale reverse osmosis desalination system, suggesting over a decade ago that it could be suitable for regions where the potable water crisis was very pressing. Sinha (2010) also found that desalination using reverse osmosis was a feasible water purification technology for these areas, being an appropriate adaptive measure in such conditions. In 2012, Shatat and Riffat explored a sustainable water purification solution through reverse osmosis technology specifically for regions where groundwater was affected by high levels of salinity. There are sustainability concerns about all forms of desalination, because of the requirement for power to drive the equipment, which is usually generated from expensive fossil fuels that produce greenhouse gases. A small laboratorial model for PV-RO (Photo-Voltaic Powered Reverse Osmosis) was designed and applied by Alkhatib in 2013 to identify its performance for seawater and brackish water. He had to do the project according to reasonable local potentialities by considering different problems. So, he applied the model to the tap water, which was close to brackish.

Reverse osmosis is a widely recognized technology for potable water shortage areas around the world and has recently been developed to a limited extent in the coastal areas of Bangladesh. However, the system also has some significant local disadvantages. It is a technologically sophisticated system which is entirely dependent on the availability of power to drive the system, and it requires the use of high pressure pumps which emit unpleasant noise. Furthermore, saline effluent discharged from desalination plants can be highly damaging for the surrounding waters, soils and ecosystems, and for the agriculture and fish on which local people rely. Consequently, more study is required to understand the potential for reverse osmosis technology in the coastal Bangladesh context.

Ahmed (1996) noted that around the Bay of Bengal, some 76 Bangladeshi upazilas (formerly known as 'thana', the second lowest tier of regional administration in the country) had experienced problems where complex hydrogeological conditions and poor water quality made water supply relatively more difficult to maintain than in other parts of the country. Low salinity surface water from ponds is normally used for drinking and domestic purposes, because in most parts of the coastal region, unlike other areas of Bangladesh, groundwater of acceptable quality is often not available either at relatively shallow depths or from deeper aquifers (Karim, 2010). Moreover, the problem appears to be worsening. A GIS application-based study on water quality in several aquifers underlying coastal areas of Bangladesh, particularly in three upazilas, i.e., Koyra, Dighalia and Paikgassha of the Khulna Division, was conducted by Rahman *et al.* (2012) between the year 2006 and 2008. From this study, critical geographical location, land relief and degree of flooding, tidal flooding and depth of the groundwater table and salt deposits, etc., were identified as key factors for the gradual increase of saline intrusion levels, leading to critical conditions in water supply systems and acute scarcity of potable water.

The Chardoani union of Patharghata upazila in the Barguna district is one example of a rural coastal area of Bangladesh where access to acceptable freshwater is problematic. The quality of groundwater in this area is poor because of saline intrusion into formerly drinkable aquifers; rain-fed ponds are now the main source of drinking water, but they are under pressure from a range of environmental conditions and adjacent land uses. A minority of people use rainwater harvesting (RWH) systems supplied by aid agencies, capturing fresh rainwater from the roofs of their individual dwellings into storage tanks for use as drinking water. However, although adjacent to the house, these yield only limited supplies and the tanks are usually small. Alternatively, Pond Sand Filters (PSF) where water from monsoon rain-fed ponds is pumped (often by hand) through a filter into a storage tank, have also been tried in the past. Typically, these systems serve 10–15 households, and have a complex double layer of filtration media including biological materials such as coconut fibre and sand to remove contaminants. However, many of these filters are not functioning effectively in recent years because of poor maintenance and difficulties of contamination removal, and the supply ponds are subject to excessive turbidity and high salt levels. Therefore, the drinking water security of this area must be improved in other ways. In such a situation, reverse osmosis technology is an appropriate option because it has an easy and affordable maintenance system and reasonable cost, it can supply drinking water to more than 100 households and, most importantly, it provides safe and freshwater.

Methodologies

This study has two main objectives: firstly, to understand the present water security status of the study area and, secondly, to evaluate the use of reverse osmosis as a solution to the water shortages experienced at the household level in coastal rural areas of Bangladesh. Both quantitative and qualitative data were used to explore the first objective.

Household questionnaire surveys were used to collect primary data directly from respondents, by trained interviewers. The survey was undertaken in April 2016, in 100 households in the Khalifarhat and Takarkhal villages of the Charduani union of Patharghata upazila, within Barguna district. The male or female head of the household was normally sought out to answer to the questions, or in their absence another adult member of the family was asked to respond.

Simultaneously, ten drinking water samples were collected from households across the study area and tested to gather indicative information about the local water chemistry. The samples were collected in laboratory-approved bottles and taken to the Barisal zonal laboratory of the Department of Public Health Engineering (DPHE) office within six hours, for fecal coliform testing using microbial filtration methods. Total Dissolved Solids (TDS), pH and chloride content of the samples were analyzed in the DPHE laboratory in Barguna.

Results and discussion

Information on water sources

The questionnaire survey demonstrated the severity of drinking water shortages in the Chardoani union of Patharghata upazila, because potable-standard aquifers are not available at suitable depths and the surface water is highly saline. The various drinking water sources used in the area are shown in Figure 1.1. Only about one in twenty (5%) of the people in the two villages are able to draw upon deep tube-well water, because of the widespread lack

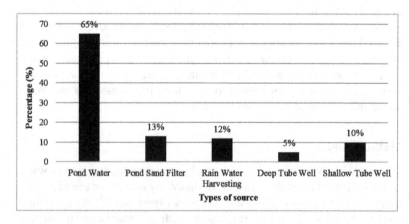

Figure 1.1 Existing drinking water sources in the study area

of suitable aquifers. About 10% of the population depends on shallow tube wells for their drinking and domestic purposes, and a further 12% people use harvested rainwater. The diagram indicates that 65% people in this area drink unfiltered pond water, with about 13% using pond sand filtration systems established by various non-governmental organizations (NGOs).

Water collection and storage system

The people in the study area follow traditional methods for collecting and storing water for drinking and domestic purposes, normally using large metallic jars. Some households use plastic pots or bottles, and a few use pottery jars for collecting and storing. Figure 1.2 shows the types of jars used for drinking water collection. With any storage vessel, there are enhanced contamination risks if it is not cleaned or sterilized regularly; contamination is particularly likely to occur with heavy pottery jars that may be semi-porous and difficult to clean. Conversely, whilst being much lighter to carry, translucent plastic containers can readily allow algae to develop on their walls.

Respondents' observations on drinking water supply

The respondents' observations on the availability of safe drinking water supplies in their communities are presented in Table 1.1. About 70% of the people are dissatisfied with the location of water sources being too far from

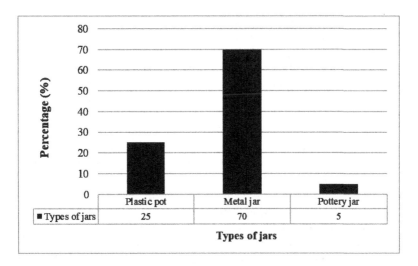

	Plastic pot	Metal jar	Pottery jar
■ Types of jars	25	70	5

Figure 1.2 Types of jars used for water collection and storage

Table 1.1 Respondents' observations on drinking water supply

Items/Variables	Satisfactory (%)	Unsatisfactory (%)
Location of water supply	30	70
Source number of water supply	25	75
Quality of pond water	15	85
Quality of tube-well water	0	100
Quality of pond sand filtering system	35	65
Quality of rainwater harvesting system	55	45
Safe water accessibility	16	84
Support from Govt./NGOs	23	77

their houses, and 75% are dissatisfied with the existing number of water sources in their community. A large majority, about 85%, are dissatisfied with the quality of pond water in their community because of salinity, hostile water quality and contamination. Only 35% of the people were satisfied with the quality of water from the local pond sand filtering systems, whereas 55% people were satisfied with the quality of their harvested rainwater, even when untreated.

More generally, 84% people were dissatisfied with the general accessibility of safe water, and most (77%) were also dissatisfied with the lack of support from government and non-governmental organizations.

Test results of water samples

The water quality test results are shown in Table 1.2, which demonstrates that there was fecal coliform contamination in several of the samples of pond-derived drinking water; this situation has frequently been observed by other researchers in rural Bangladesh. All of the pond-derived samples taken in Takarkhal exhibit fecal contamination, an indication that human sewage or animal wastes are entering the water. It is possible, but less likely, that the contamination derived from unclean storage vessels, but nevertheless it is liable to cause chronic or acute gastric and intestinal illnesses amongst those who drink the water without treating it through boiling or disinfection.

All samples of water lie within the normal range of pH in natural freshwater, with an average pH of 7.39; groundwater from the tube wells in Takarkhal is somewhat more alkaline, whereas the harvested rainwater is slightly acidic. All would be acceptable for drinking on this basis.

The test results of Total Dissolved Solid (TDS) and chloride are shown in the below Figure 1.3, where sample-8 and sample-9 contain higher levels of TDS and chloride than the normal range. Sample-8 holds 1450 mg/l TDS and 840 mg/l chloride and sample-9 holds 1280 mg/l TDS and 720 mg/l Chloride,

Table 1.2 Test results of water samples

No. of sample*	Name of the area	GPS coordinate	Water collection source	Fecal coliform** (n/100 ml)	pH	TDS (mg/ litre)	Chloride (mg/ litre)
Sample-1	Khalifarhat	N-22.06884 E-089.91977	Pond	0	6.5	850	300
Sample-2	Khalifarhat	N-22.06878 E-089.92123	Pond	**2**	6.8	780	240
Sample-3	Khalifarhat	N-22.07002 E-089.92188	Pond	0	7.3	646	180
Sample-4	Khalifarhat	N-22.10809 E-089.92167	RWH	0	6.5	380	80
Sample-5	Khalifarhat	N-22.10465 E-089.92059	PSF	0	7.2	665	180
Sample-6	Takarkhal	N-22.10430 E-089.93872	Pond	**12**	7.5	560	260
Sample-7	Takarkhal	N-22.10603 E-089.93929	Pond	**16**	7.4	885	280
Sample-8	Takarkhal	N-22.10864 E-089.93944	SDT	0	8.6	**1450**	**840**
Sample-9	Takarkhal	N-22.10885 E-089.93943	DT	0	8.3	**1280**	**720**
Sample-10	Takarkhal	N-22.10917 E-089.93943	Pond	**12**	7.8	780	240

* Samples were collected on August 4, 2016.
** Concentration of fecal coliform into water was identified in number per 100 millilitres through the microbial filtration method (MFM).
*** Bold format indicates that the testing results are higher than the standard range in Bangladesh. The standard range of fecal coliform is "0", TDS is "1000 mg/l" and chloride is "150–600 mg/l" for drinking water according to Bangladesh standards and WHO guidelines.

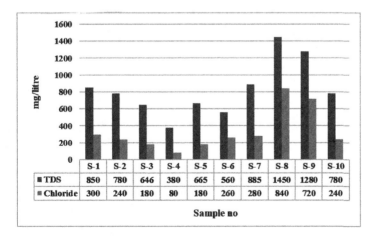

Figure 1.3 Test results of TDS and chloride

respectively. According to Bangladesh standards and WHO guidelines, the standard range of TDS is 1,000 mg/l and the standard range of chloride is 150–600 mg/l for drinking water (DPHE, 2016). According to the water sample test results, it was found that about 60% households in the study area have poor quality water, and consequently a serious problem of water insecurity.

Feasibility of reverse osmosis desalination plant

If a reverse osmosis desalination plant were to be built in the study area, it could potentially play a role in improving the water security of this area, but to be practical the system would also need to be technically and economically feasible in the longer term. The feasibility of reverse osmosis systems is critically dependent on location and the availability of a reliable electricity supply. Electricity is available in the study area, and a small-scale reverse osmosis plant was installed by the authors in March 2016, with financial support from the Department of Public Health Engineering, Barguna to solve the water shortages problem.

To properly evaluate economic feasibility, a generalized method of assessing the economics of small-scale reverse osmosis systems was developed, comparing the development costs of the desalination system, conventional pond sand filters, and rainwater harvesting. The results of this generalized feasibility study are briefly summarized below. Here Table 1.3 shows a reverse osmosis plant analysis, with some of the input parameters.

Cost analysis of a reverse osmosis plant

Total system cost of a reverse osmosis desalination plant is given below (Table 1.4).

Table 1.5 shows the detailed comparative analysis of the three systems, with some input parameters based on installation cost, plant lifetime and coverage of households. As those areas have higher water shortages, the economical and long-lasting system will be technically feasible for strengthening water security for the coastal region.

Table 1.3 Feasibility assessment of a reverse osmosis plant at the study area

Parameter	Value
Capacity of installed RO plant	1800–2000 litres/hour
Lifetime of the RO plant	25–30 years
Recovery ratio of the plant	65%
Coverage household	100 (approximate)
Total setup cost	Approximately 3,200 USD

Table 1.4 Cost analysis of a reverse osmosis plant

Item	Cost (USD)
Setup cost (pretreatment filter, posttreatment filter)	1,200
Membrane cost	150
Storage tank	300
Pump cost	150
Brine disposal cost	350
House building cost for plant setup	600
Labor cost	350
Others cost (transport, logistics, service charge, etc.)	100
Total system cost of a reverse osmosis desalination plant	3,200 USD

The average household cost of setting up a RO plant is:
Total system cost/number of households = ($3,200 / 100) = $32 (approximate)

Table 1.5 Comparative analysis of RO, PSF and RWH (DPHE, 2016)

System Name	RO Plant	RWH	PSF
Installation cost (approx.)	3,200 USD	650 USD	1,500 USD
Plant lifetime	25–30 years	15–20 years	10–15 years
Coverage of households	100 households	1 household	10 households
Cost per household	32 USD	650 USD	150 USD

The feasibility assessment of RO analysis and comparative analysis results of RO, PSF and RWH systems show that the reverse osmosis system is economically and technically feasible for this coastal region. Although costs are very high to establish an RO plant, considering the supply capacity of water, costs are comparatively low for an individual household as such a plant can provide safe and freshwater to more than 100 households.

In fact, conventional pond sand filters (PSF) and rainwater harvesting systems are not economically feasible due to higher installation costs to cover all the households. To strengthen water security using the rainwater harvesting system, each household in the study area would need the system installed, which would be very costly for government or non-governmental organizations. Additionally, this system would not provide safe drinking water all year round because of its low storage tank.

This study reveals that the PSF system for safe drinking water supply is very difficult to implement in the coastal area of Bangladesh. It cannot remove all bacterial contamination. Also, there are now many inactive PSF plants due to technical problems and scarcity of rainwater during the dry season. Therefore, it is clear that an additional source of safe drinking water is an urgent need for coastal Bangladesh.

Conclusion

The different test results of water samples indicate that the water security status of the coastal area is very poor. For this reason, the RO system can be one of the desirable sources of drinking water for coastal people, to achieve the goal of sustainable development (SDG 6) on 'water and sanitation'. This system is a technically and economically feasible option to mitigate the water shortage problem. The installed RO plant's water sample test result shows that the quality of the reverse osmosis water is very good to drink, satisfactory and absolutely free from harmful substances. It can play a great role in fulfiling people's daily drinking water demand at the household level in coastal rural areas of Bangladesh.

Acknowledgements

The authors are grateful to Professor Dr. Muhammad Maniruzzaman, Department of Agricultural Chemistry, Patuakhali Science and Technology University and Mr. Mohammed Mahmud Khan, Executive Engineer, Department of Public Health Engineering (DPHE), Barguna, Bangladesh for their constructive guidance and valuable suggestions during the research process. The authors also wish to thank the organizing members of the second Annual Conference on Sustainable Development (2017) at the University of Liberal Arts Bangladesh (ULAB) for their support and cooperation.

References

Ahmed, M. F. (1996). *Coastal Water Supply in Bangladesh, Reaching the Unreached: Challenges for the 21st Century*. Proceedings of 22nd WEDC Conference, New Delhi, India.

Alkhatib, A. (2013). Reverse-osmosis desalination of water powered by photovoltaic modules. *Computational Water, Energy, and Environmental Engineering, 3*(1), 22. DOI: 10.4236/cweee.2014.31003

Basar, A. (2012). Water security in coastal region of Bangladesh: Would desalination be a solution to the vulnerable communities of the Sundarbans? *Bangladesh e-Journal of Sociology, 9*(2), 31.

Cheah, S. F. (2004). *Photovoltaic Reverse Osmosis Desalination System*. US Department of the Interior, Bureau of Reclamation, Denver Office, Technical Service Center, Environmental Services Division, Water Treatment Engineering and Research Group.

Cotruvo, J., Voutchkov, N., Fawell, J., Payment, P., Cunliffe, D., & Lattemann, S. (Eds.). (2010). *Desalination Technology: Health and Environmental Impacts*. CRC Press, Taylor & Francis Group, Boca Raton, Florida.

Department of Public Health Engineering (DPHE). (2016). *Water Quality Parameters Bangladesh Standards & WHO Guide Lines*. Department of Public Health

Engineering, Government of Peoples Republic of Bangladesh. Retrieved from http://dphe.gov.bd/index.php?option=com_content&view=article&id=125&Ite mid=1

Garud, R. M., Kore, S. V., Kore, V. S., & Kulkarni, G. S. (2011). A short review on process and applications of reverse osmosis. *Universal Journal of Environmental Research & Technology*, *1*(3), 233–238.

Gleick, P. H. (1993). Water and conflict: Fresh water resources and international security. *International Security*, *18*(1), 79–112. DOI: 10.2307/2539033

Islam, M. R., & Ahmad, M. (2004). *Living in the Coast: Problems, Opportunities and Challenges*. Program Development Office for Integrated Coastal Zone Management Plan Project. Water Resources Planning Organization. Dhaka, Bangladesh.

Karim, M. R. (2010). Assessment of rainwater harvesting for drinking water supply in Bangladesh. *Water Science and Technology: Water Supply*, *10*(2), 243–249. DOI: 10.2166/ws.2010.896

Khanom, S., & Salehin, M. (2012). Salinity constraints to different water uses in coastal area of Bangladesh: A case study. *Bangladesh Journal of Scientific Research*, *25*(1), 33–41. http://dx.doi.org/10.3329/bjsr.v25i1.13048

Rahman, M., Ahmeduzzaman, M., & Zahir, H. (2012). A study on the water quality at different aquifers of Khulna district: A GIS application. *International Journal of Engineering Research and Applications*, *2*(6), 1202–1207.

Shatat, M., & Riffat, S. B. (2012). Water desalination technologies utilizing conventional and renewable energy sources. *International Journal of Low-Carbon Technologies*, *9*(1), 1–19. https://doi.org/10.1093/ijlct/cts025

Shrimali, H. V. (2015). A brief review on reverse osmosis technology. *International Journal of Research in Advent Technology*, *3*(5), 93–97.

Sinha, R. K. (2010). *Desalination & Water Purification Technologies*. Government of India, Mumbai.

Wingender, J., & Flemming, H. C. (2011). Biofilms in drinking water and their role as reservoir for pathogens. *International Journal of Hygiene and Environmental Health*, *214*(6), 417–423. https://doi.org/10.1016/j.ijheh.2011.05.009

Part 2

Sustainable Development Goal 7

Affordable and clean energy

2 Application of sustainable energy paradigm through solar bottle light

A case study from Dhaka, Bangladesh

Md. Jakariya, Sajid Iqbal, Navojit Dastidar and Mohammad Sujauddin

Introduction

Human greed and aspirations have led to battles and wars since the beginning of civilization. Natural resource extraction and energy consumption have escalated as nations and corporations have competed, either by invading other nations, by advancement in science and technology or through annexation of new territories for various natural sources of energy. China alone consumed 3,034 million tons of oil equivalent (Mtoe) energy in 2014 (Enerdata, 2015). Alternative sources of renewable energy are being developed, albeit slowly; thirty years may not be sufficient to switch from fossil fuel to clean energy, since development of newer alternative energy production at a large scale takes a long time. Fossil fuel consumption also comes with severe health repercussions. The World Health Organization (WHO) estimated that in 2012 seven million people died from air pollution, making this cause one out of every eight deaths in the world (WHO, 2012). Hence there is a second imperative for reducing reliance on fossil fuel-derived sources of energy.

Densely populated developing countries such as Bangladesh have their own share of energy-related problems. Bangladesh is now considered to be a lower-middle income country, according to the World Bank (2015). With the rising purchasing power of the middle class and burgeoning rural to urban migration, energy demand is rising. According to the Bangladesh Power Development Board (BPDB) (2012), industrial and agricultural sectors accounted for 45% of electricity consumption in Bangladesh from 1995 to 2010, with 55% consumed by domestic users. Supply of electricity is inadequate for the growing demand, and further economic growth is hindered by the weak electricity infrastructure. Though per capita consumption has increased from 11 kilowatt hours (kWh) in 1971 to 293 kWh in 2013, Bangladesh still ranks as one of the lowest electricity-consuming countries in the world (World Bank, 2014a). Beyond that, hardship is experienced by millions of city (especially slum) dwellers who suffer from power outages for three to four hours every day.

Clean alternative energy sources have now penetrated the Bangladeshi energy market. As of 2014, the World Bank reported that with 70,000 solar home systems being installed every month, Bangladesh was experiencing the fastest rise in such installations in the world. To further encourage this endeavour, the World Bank lent Bangladesh $78.4 million (World Bank, 2014b). Infrastructure Development Company Ltd. (IDCOL) reported that 3.1 million solar photovoltaic home systems were installed until May 2014, with a capacity of 140 MW electricity, sufficient to provide clean energy for 14 million rural people at current levels of use (IDCOL, 2014). However, energy challenges also continue to bear down on the urban slum population. The city of Dhaka now contains more than 18 million people (World Bank, 2017) packed into some 816 square kilometers. Approximately 500,000 more migrants arrive every year (Khan, 2009), putting additional strain on the thinly stretched networks of energy supply within the city. Installation of solar home systems is not an option for the majority as most occupy densely packed slums and squats with tin roofs with minimal ventilation or penetration of sunlight during the day. Hence they depend on high power (60W) light bulbs even in daylight hours. The electricity connections acquired by these impoverished inhabitants, typically from nearby electric poles used to run electricity cables for established houses, are not only dangerous and illegal, but also lead to frequent load shedding. A similar situation also applies, albeit less acutely, to the rural population of Bangladesh.

The rate at which sustainable energy, particularly with distributed generation, is embraced, therefore appears crucial. However, many of the widely used sustainable energy sources such as wind power (Twidell & Weir, 2015), solar thermal technology, hydropower, geothermal energy and biomass (Herzog *et al.*, 2001) are relatively costly (M. J., 2014), so there is a pressing need concurrently to reduce consumption. Innovation has led to the invention of an inexpensive and environmentally friendly device known as the "solar bottle light" (SBL), which lights up these shacks during the day using sunlight, but about which very little research has been done. Attached to the tin roofs of slum property, this "energy in a bottle" can potentially brighten up living space and save energy, freeing people from a level of hopelessness. In line with the United Nations Sustainable Development Goal 7, our study is an attempt to evaluate the application of SBLs in the slums of Bangladesh as a sustainable means to secure clean and affordable energy.

Background of the solar bottle light

The inventor of SBL was Alfredo Moser, an impoverished Brazilian mechanic who worked indoors and needed an alternative low-cost source of light to the existing electric light bulbs. Making use of refraction, the bending of light, it travels through mediums of varied densities, Moser went on to invent an

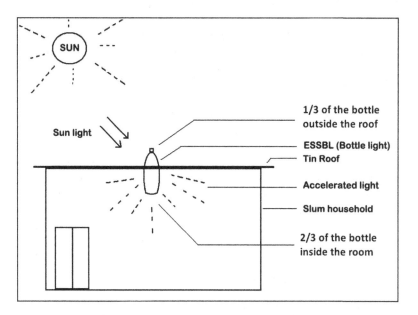

Figure 2.1 SBL diagram

inexpensive light source using recycled plastic drink bottles. Also known as "Moser lamp," these SBLs emit light equivalent to a 40–60 Watt electric bulb, depending on the availability and intensity of sunlight (Zobel, 2013).

The chief building materials of SBL are widely available scrap tin, and large clean plastic bottles filled with water. The bottle is then attached to the tin roof using a waterproof adhesive such as silicon glue, purchased from hardware shops. Despite minor differences in materials used in Bangladesh, the installation process is largely similar to the one undertaken by Moser. "Botul bati" gained popularity in Bangladesh's Baonea-Badh slum very quickly in about 2002; "botul" in Bengali means bottle and "bati" represents lamp/light. The present cost of an SBL can range from BDT 250 (USD 2.99) to BDT 300 with installation charges. The minimum installation charge is BDT 100, with the majority of its cost attributable to the silicon glue which costs BDT 160 per 300 ml cartridge. From this research, it has been established that two people can install up to 10 SBLs per day. Figure 2.1 shows a schematic diagram of an SBL.

Methodology

Funded by the German development agency, Deutsche Gesellschaft für Internationale Zusammenarbeit (GIZ), the test installation of SBLs in Bangladesh took place between April and August 2013, in the shanty town of

Baonea-Badh, in the Northern Mirpur area of the capital city of Dhaka. Baonea-Badh is typical of other recently occupied Dhaka areas, and contains approximately 900 immigrant households with an average of some four residents per household. It is an emerging slum where small "cottage" businesses, development schools, Madrassas, mechanics and scrap shops and other small retail outlets sit alongside poor quality and crowded living spaces. Construction is generally flimsy, usually tin roofs with concrete blocks, wood panels or plastic sheeting walls. Sanitation is limited, and most premises are heavily dependent on illegal electricity connections to illuminate the indoor working and living spaces. Candles are also used, with an associated fire risk and damage to occupants' health from fumes. The study covered approximately 15% of the households, with baseline research revealing that each household used an average of 1.32 electric light bulbs for ten hours per day to illuminate income-generating work such as making *saree* (an Indigenous cloth produced mainly by women) or repairing rickshaws, activities such as childrens' education and household tasks.

To analyze the impact of SBLs, the project was implemented in two phases. Firstly, baseline data was collected from seventy randomly selected households, before commencement of the main installation phases of the project in April 2013. SBLs were installed in 250 households, after which information was collected from a randomly selected 30% of the recipients by interview in July 2013. SPSS statistics 17.0 and Microsoft Excel were used for statistical analysis of the data.

Result and discussion

Acceptance of SBL in the study area

The study revealed that, upon installation of the SBLs, approximately 83% of the recipient Baonea-Badh households reduced their daytime reliance on electric light bulbs. The acceptance rate of the SBLs was impressive. Initially, the entire concept of SBL was virtually unknown to the slum dwellers, hence a series of door-to-door promotional campaigns were initiated about 10 days before the scheduled start of the installation process, to raise awareness. During this period, residents were observed to be very interested in the possibilities of the new technology, and they approached the project with optimism, enthusiasm and responsibility. Initially, residents were unwilling to pay for an installation, but as the benefits were gradually realized they began paying from USD 0.24 to USD 0.48. By the time the installation target was reached, many residents were willing to pay up to USD 0.60, despite a planned reduction in the frequency of promotion. The overall rising trend in demand for the SBL, along with the decreasing campaign frequency (shown in Figure 2.2 below), demonstrates the increasingly positive attitude

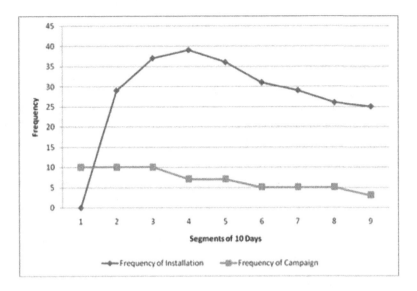

Figure 2.2 Relationship between campaign frequency and demand of the bottle light

displayed by the slum dwellers. Various key factors such as higher literacy rate and greater income are assumed to be the drivers of such an acceptance rate in the Baonea-Badh slum in comparison to other adjacent slums.

Energy conservation and carbon emissions reduction

Table 2.1 shows calculations of the reduction of energy consumption and carbon emissions in recipient households in the Baonea-Badh area. These are then used to project the potential total reduction in energy consumption and carbon emissions from the entire slum population of Bangladesh, assuming widespread adoption of the SBL. It is assumed that the carbon emissions are the result of electricity generation by mostly natural gas, as it accounts for over half of all electricity generated in Bangladesh (Wadud *et al.*, 2011).

The massive potential of SBLs is apparent. In fact, even more could be done to save electricity and air pollution in Bangladesh if the principles of light refraction in an SBL were used at a larger scale in factories and industries. This technology could also be applied in other countries where rampant slum growth has been experienced, for example, India, South Africa, Kenya, Pakistan and Mexico. In the Philippines, 382,000 residents have already benefited from the use of SBLs through persistent effort by "Liter of Light", a development charity now operating globally (Climate Heroes, 2015).

Table 2.1 Energy conservation and carbon emissions reduction by using SBLs

Factors	Numeric values	Unit	Energy reduction
Energy conservation			
Number of light bulbs/household	1.32	60 W	792 Wh
Length of usage/day/household	10	hours	
Households with continued SBL	208	–	165 kWh/day
Total reduction/month (study area)			4.94 MWh
Total reduction of electricity usage	592,998[a]		171.4G Wh
from the entire slum population of	365	days	
Bangladesh/year			
Reduction of carbon emissions			***CO₂ reduction***
Emissions/kWh	513[b]	grams	2534 kg
Monthly electricity reduction	4.94	MWh/	
(study area)		month	
Total reduction in CO_2 emissions	171.4	GWh	**87.9 million MT**
from the entire slum population of			
Bangladesh/year			

a BBS (2015)
b IEA (2011)

Estimation of effective carbon dioxide reduction

The scenario-based estimates proposed in Table 2.2 are aligned with several different Bangladeshi environmental and cultural factors. These factors include a mix of various religious and cultural festivals, and seasonal changes in the climate. Scenario 1 describes a situation where sunlight is available at a constant high rate throughout the year, and all slum households are accepting of the SBLs. The remaining scenarios are developed in comparison to this scenario. Scenario 2 corrects for the shanty town residents returning to their home villages for a month of traditional annual holidays, and Scenario 3 allows for the climatological impacts of reduced rainy and winter season sunlight availability. Due to the existence of these exogenous factors, it is apparent that 100% effectiveness will most likely not be achieved; Scenarios 2 and 3 are in reality inevitable, with the climatological impacts being greater than those resulting from cultural practices. Consequently, the energy savings will not be as high, because the impact of domestic holidays when people return to villages will affect SBL use in city slums, and climatological impacts will affect the availability of strong sunlight. Scenario 4 amalgamates these two effects, providing a more likely estimate of SBL use impacts and suggesting that in total about 52% of the potential total energy savings might actually be realized.

Table 2.2 Establishing different scenarios to estimate the effective rate of carbon dioxide reduction based on endemic situations

Scenarios	Explanation	Estimated rate of effectiveness
Scenario 1	This is the base-scenario. It is the ideal situation where the sunlight is available at a constant rate throughout the year and all slum households are accepting of the SBLs. The following scenarios are developed in comparison to this scenario.	100%
Scenario 2	Approximately one month of public holidays per year is observed in Bangladesh when people in cities retreat to their village hometowns to spend joyous occasions/festivals like Eid and Puja with their families. At this instance, a number of city slum dwellers can also be expected to leave their slums to head back to their village residence. Hence SBL usage during this month can be expected to fall.	92%
Scenario 3	Bangladesh experiences six different seasons where the rainy season and winter last for two months each. During these four months, excessive clouds and fog may reduce sunlight penetration to the Earth's surface during the day by a certain amount. Lower intensity of sunlight would hamper the effectiveness of the SBL. As a result, more people may turn to electric lights during these four months.	60%
Scenario 4	(100% – Scenario 2) + (100% – Scenario 3)	52%

Detailed information on the annual cycle of slum-household occupation in Bangladesh, specific levels of sunlight received during each season and a complete census of slum dwellers' opinions of the SBL would enable greater precision in the estimates. The true essence of Figure 2.3 is the realization that, since it is virtually impossible to reach the ideal base-scenario where effectiveness is at 100%, high levels of carbon reduction can only be achieved with sheer determination and aggressiveness towards spreading the use of SBLs.

Economic and social benefits

The economic and social benefits of SBLs are considerable. Greater visibility in homes and businesses has health and safety benefits, and allows for domestic activities such as cleaning and cooking to take place more

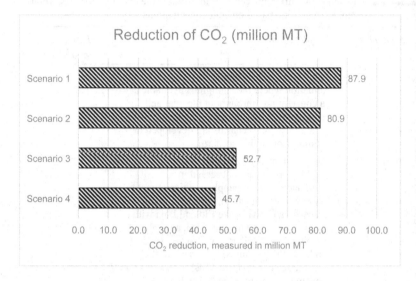

Figure 2.3 Estimation of effective carbon dioxide reduction

easily. Replacing the use of light bulbs with SBLs also helped to reduce room temperatures, typically by almost 1.5 degree Celsius during the day, promoting a more comfortable interior environment for the residents. The impact of power outages or load shedding no longer posed such a serious threat to normal living and working life during daylight hours. Moreover, people attempting to secure illicit and dangerous connections to electricity sources declined significantly during the course of the project.

Baonea-Badh slum residents who own small businesses have particularly benefited from the SBLs as many of them previously depended on using electric light during the day. The system helped them to reduce their usage of electricity for about 10 hours each day, which reduced their bills by an estimated USD 2.57–3.85 per month. In practice, fewer bulbs would also need to be purchased. This releases money for other uses such as paying for their children's educational needs and allowing the completion of school homework in the dwelling. These bottle lights have also led to multiplier effects in residents' developing additional sources of income. For example, a rickshaw puller can generate some additional income by making and selling the accessories which are required for installation and maintenance for the SBLs, using recycled materials. In terms of economic benefits, the viability and widespread willingness of cottage industry and small business owners to use SBL in their small shops reduces cost, hence raising profit.

Challenges of implementation and usage of SBLs

Challenges with the use of SBLs nevertheless arose throughout the project period, manifested in complaints from residents about the performance of the systems, and in their feelings about their use.

* 20% of the users of SBLs complained of excess lighting causing distur-bance to periods of sleep during daylight hours on sunny days, because the system cannot be "switched off". This affected both adults taking daytime naps (including shift workers), and young children. As a result, a black cloth cover had to be used to cover-up the light when required.
* 2.5% to 3% of the installations developed leaks when observed monthly for a period after installation, allowing rainwater on the roof to seep inside the dwellings. Thus, stronger sealants and more highly trained users are required to install or repair these lights. It is also unclear what the life expectancy of the systems will be, if water, plastic bottles or sealants need replacing as they slowly degrade.
* The efficacy of SBLs remain limited only to daytime use, whilst little has been done improve the situation in the slums at night. The solu-tion to this issue has been addressed by MyShelter Foundation (Krish-namurthy, 2014) in the Philippines by immersing a waterproof circuit in an SBL, containing a small LED light that lights up at the absence of sunlight. A light dependent resistor attached to the bottle cap and the circuit detects the lack of sunlight, which then lights up the LED light inside the SBL. Philosophically, the United Nations Development Goal 7, on "access to affordable, reliable, sustainable and modern energy for all", is achieved only in part by using SBLs since the energy harvesting systems are not "modern" in the sense originally implied in the text of the Goal and cannot address the need for interior light at night time. SBLs are perhaps an interim solution, in this sense, prior to a longer term and more complete solution to the lack of sustainable power in slums. They nevertheless have advantages.
* Related to this, some of the patrons of SBLs explained that mentally they felt poorer as they were using makeshift lights made from recycled materials rather than the more technologically sophisticated electric light bulbs. The project raised challenges around aspirations, as well as securing some improvement in slum residents' day-to-day experiences.

Conclusion and policy implications

The principal socio-economic benefits of SBL use include the enhancement of slum dwellers' living standards, the reduction in the use of illegal sources of electricity, the overall reduction in electricity usage and the potential major decline in carbon emissions (by 2,534 kg per month, assuming wide take-up). Beyond that, the system could reduce electricity bills by up to USD 4 per month for cottage industry electricity users; electricity bills currently take a disproportionately large amount of slum residents' incomes. Since cottage industries involve many female workers, improved profitability of this sector would potentially also encourage female entrepreneurship and empowerment.

Problems regarding hardware choice and sound maintenance of the SBLs during severe stormy weather and hurricanes pose a threat to the long-term sustainability of the system, alongside the challenges discussed above. Beyond that, educating slum residents to understand their own influence on the environment is yet another obstacle, even though their impact is likely to be very small in comparison with that of wealthier residents in Dhaka and beyond. This opens opportunities for further research and development work on improving the materials of SBLs and also providing motivational material and environmental literacy to the residents. Simplification of the challenges discussed above would heighten the possibilities of merits from SBL usage. The results derived from this study suggest that countries with similar demographic and geographic attributes could use SBLs to light up the houses of impoverished people and reduce national carbon footprints simultaneously.

It is essential to note that, given the tendency of impoverished slum residents to be cautious about potential lifestyle changes, as a result in part of lack of education and a conservative mindset, the propagation of SBLs throughout the entire slum population of Bangladesh could take a very long time. In the words of the former CEO of Exxon Mobil Corporation, Rex Tillerson:

> When coal came into the picture, it took about 50 or 60 years to displace timber. Then, crude oil was found, and it took 60, 70 years, and then natural gas. So it takes 100 years or more for some new breakthrough in energy to become the dominant source. Most people have difficulty coming to grips with the sheer enormity of energy consumption.

In other words, changes away from traditional sources of light and energy must be embraced without delay. Holding the inelastic nature of energy consumption as an excuse to veer away from clean and affordable alternatives to fossil fuels is not acceptable. In fact, if we choose to factor in the inelasticity of energy demand and supply, we need to consider deploying small and grassroots-level changes, such as the SBL, immediately. This could partly be achieved through governmental assistance, where the government could mandate the usage of SBLs in slum areas, similar to the implementation of compulsory solar home panels on the roofs of every residential building.

Acknowledgement

The authors would like to thank Mr. Jan Söhlemann, Monitoring Adviser, Sustainable Energy for Development (SED) Programme, Deutsche Gesellschaft für Internationale Zusammenarbeit (GIZ).

References

Bangladesh Power Development Board. (2012). *Bangladesh Power Development Board Website*. Retrieved from www.bpdb.gov.bd/bpdb/

BBS. (2015). *Preliminary Report on Census of Slum Areas and Floating Population 2014*. Dhaka: Bangladesh Bureau of Statistics. Retrieved from http://203.112.218.65:8008/WebTestApplication/userfiles/Image/Slum/Preli_Slum_Census.pdf

Climate Heroes. (2015). *Climate Heroes*. Retrieved from www.climateheroes.org

Enerdata. (2015). *Total Energy Consumption*. Historical Stagnation in Energy Consumption. Retrieved from https://yearbook.enerdata.net/

Herzog, A. V., Lipman, T. E., & Kammen, D. M. (2001). Renewable energy sources. *Encyclopedia of Life Support Systems (EOLSS)*. Perspectives and Overview of Life Support Systems and Sustainable Development. Retrieved from: http://rael.berkeley.edu/old_drupal/sites/default/files/old-site-files/2001/Herzog-Lipman-Kammen-RenewableEnergy-2001.pdf

IEA. (2011). *CO_2 Emissions From Fuel Combustion Highlights*. Paris: International Energy Agency.

Infrastructure Development Company Limited [IDCOL]. (2014). *IDCOL Wins the Karlsruhe Sustainable Finance Award 2014*. Retrieved from http://idcol.org/home/news_details/84

Khan, M. S. (2009). *Migration in Dhaka*. Retrieved from http://archive.thedailystar.net/newDesign/news-details.php?nid=106930

Krishnamurthy, R. (2014). *Solar Water Bottle Bulbs*. Retrieved from http://permaculturenews.org/2014/03/14/solar-water-bottle-bulbs/

M. J. (2014). *Why Is Renewable Energy so Expensive?* Retrieved from www.economist.com/blogs/economist-explains/2014/01/economist-explains-0

Twidell, J., & Weir, T. (2015). *Renewable Energy Resources*. Abingdon, UK: Routledge.

Wadud, Z., Dey, H. S., Kabir, M. A., & Khan, S. I. (2011). Modeling and forecasting natural gas demand in Bangladesh. *Energy Policy, 39*(11), 7372–7380.

World Bank. (2014a). *Electric Power Consumption* (kWh per Capita). Retrieved from http://data.worldbank.org/indicator/EG.USE.ELEC.KH.PC

World Bank. (2014b). *Bangladesh Receives $78.4 Million to Install an Additional 480,000 Solar Home Systems*. Retrieved from www.worldbank.org/en/news/press-release/2014/06/30/bangladesh-receives-usd-78-million-to-install-an-additional-480000-solar-home-systems

World Bank. (2015). *WB Update Says 10 Countries Move Up in Income Bracket*. Retrieved from www.worldbank.org/en/news/press-release/2015/07/01/new-worldbank-update-shows-bangladesh-kenya-myanmar-and-tajikistan-as-middle-income-while-south-sudan-falls-back-to-low-income

World Bank. (2017). *Toward Great Dhaka.* Retrieved from www.worldbank.org/en/news/speech/2017/07/19/toward-great-dhaka

World Health Organization. (2012). *7 Million Premature Deaths Annually Linked to Air Pollution.* Retrieved from www.who.int/mediacentre/news/releases/2014/air-pollution/en/

Zobel, G. (2013). *Alfredo Moser: Bottle Light Inventor Proud to Be Poor.* Retrieved from www.bbc.com/news/magazine-23536914

Part 3

Sustainable Development Goal 12

Ensure sustainable consumption and production

3 Feasibility of solar-biomass hybrid cold storage for unelectrified rural areas of Bangladesh

Priyanka Chowdhury, Andrew Jenkins and Zainu Sadia Islam

Introduction

It was estimated in 2011 that roughly one-third of all food produced for human consumption was lost or wasted, accounting for about 1.3 billion metric tons of food per annum (Food and Agriculture Organization (FAO), 2011). It was also assessed that post-harvest losses amounted to between 24% and 40% on average in developing countries, and between 2% and 20% in developed countries. This is clearly a major challenge in relation to Sustainable Development Goal (SDG) 12: "Ensure sustainable consumption and production patterns". The percentage of post-harvest losses is considerably higher when proper storage and cooling facilities are absent (Bangladesh Rehabilitation Assistance Committee [BRAC] & SEFA, 2015). Therefore, an urgent need exists to extend the period of availability for perishable foodstuffs.

In Bangladesh it has been found that the post-harvest loss of fruits and vegetables ranges from 23.6% to 43.5% with a monetary value of BDT 34,420 million (USD 445 million) (Hassan *et al.*, 2010). About 70% of the people in Bangladesh live in rural areas, and grid electricity is available for only 40% of them (World Bank [WB], 2014). Considering this situation, storage powered by a hybrid of solar and biomass energy is a fruitful area for exploration, since biomass is a widely available source of renewable energy for electricity generation. Moreover, in the field of solar energy, electricity generation is getting cheaper day by day. Previous studies on this innovative solution have been done both in India and Spain. This can be an interesting matter to look into, if we consider the diverse socio-economic backgrounds of the stakeholders involved in the agricultural process and the diversity of geographic areas within Bangladesh. If such a model is found to be feasible and locally acceptable to the farmers and other stakeholders, then we can further plan the implementation, incorporating this model into the existing models of the USAID Horticulture Project in Bangladesh, funded by USAID and implemented jointly by the International Potato Center (CIP) and BRAC. BRAC, an international development organization based in Bangladesh, is the largest non-governmental development organization in the world, in terms of number of employees as of September 2016. Established by Sir Fazle Hasan Abed in 1972 after the independence of Bangladesh, BRAC is present in all 64 districts of Bangladesh as well as 13 other countries in Asia, Africa and the Americas.

This feasibility study focused on the cold storage of potatoes in Bangladesh, since it is currently a crucial source of nutrition in Bangladeshi diets and calories are needed to meet the needs of a growing population. Bangladesh has achieved a surplus in potato production, but there is still a need for both short-term and long-term local storage since a lot of production is currently wasted (Hossain & Miah, 2009). Although the estimated postharvest loss of potatoes in Bangladesh lacks empirical research, findings by Katalyst (Egger, n.d.) suggest that the loss is significant.

This study focused on a 20-ton cold storage facility. A similar model based on a hybrid between solar and biomass energy has already been tested successfully in India. This model was used as an exemplar, with adjustments made to fit it into the context of Bangladesh; data from India was collected and analyzed as well as data from relevant farmers in Bangladesh and relevant technical information from key informants in the Netherlands. The study is aligned with United Nations Sustainable Development Goal (SDG) 7, "Affordable and clean energy". Investments need to be made in clean energy sources such as solar, wind and thermal to ensure universal access to affordable electricity by 2030. SDG 7 also asserts that "Expanding infrastructure and upgrading technology to provide clean energy in all developing countries is a crucial goal that can both encourage growth and help the environment" (United Nations Development Programme [UNDP], 2017). The objectives of this study are hence (1) to analyze the economic and technical feasibility of the existing models and propose a new model for Bangladesh, if feasible, and (2) to identify the potential scope for implementing solar-biomass hybrid cold storage in rural Bangladesh.

Material and methods

In Bangladesh it was necessary to understand the off-grid cold storage requirements of farmers and traders, so purposive sampling was used amongst potato farmers and traders. Focus groups were selected to gain the opinions of many stakeholders in the upazila of Piragacha (Rangpur district) within the given time constraints. Bangladesh has some 500 upazilas, which are the second lowest tier of regional administration in Bangladesh. Two focus group discussions were conducted. The first focus group was with potato farmers of the upazila. The second focus group was with a group of seed and potato traders. Participants, particularly men, were selected according to the predetermined criterion that they were at least 20 years old. The sample included resident farmers and traders in order to get a comprehensive and insightful perspective of the current extent of potato loss and the existence of cold storage facilities. The use of BRAC local field staff ensured a representative group of local people. They included the participants using a "snowball sampling technique", which entailed a suitable farmer helping to contact and draw in another suitable farmer.

For the in-depth interviews (IDIs), farmers residing in the Pirgacha area were identified by BRAC staff of the corresponding locality. As many as possible IDIs were conducted until data saturation occurred. A total of seven IDIs were conducted among farmers in Pirgacha, Rangpur. Topics covered in the IDIs included the current extent of perishable food loss, especially potato loss and cold storage facilities. This study additionally focused on identifying the current availability of cooling storage facilities and the future possibility of introducing solar and biomass hybrid cold storage facilities

For the key informant interviews (KIIs), institutional heads, programme coordinators and project managers were interviewed in Bangladesh, India and the Netherlands. A total of 14 KIIs were conducted in order to capture the expert opinions on the various players operating at various points in the supply chain. The following sources were interviewed: solar and biomass companies (national and international), cold storage companies (national and international), cold storage facilities (Rangpur district) and potato farmers (Rangpur district). Out of these, a total of eight KIIs were undertaken among various stakeholders in Bangladesh, such as BRAC Cold Storage, BRAC Solar, IDCOL, Solaric, Rahima Ferooz, Cold Storage Association, Grameen Shakti and the cold storage in Rangpur. Four KIIs were conducted in India with The Energy and Resources Institute (TERI), NISE and Thermax.

Methodology of economic feasibility calculations

In order to determine the economic feasibility of the different models, net present value (NPV) and levelized cost of electricity (LCOE) calculations were made. The NPV and LCOE were computed with the following formulas:

$$NPV = \sum_{t=1}^{T} \left(\frac{CF_t}{(1+r)^t} \right)$$

$$LCOE = \frac{I + \left(\sum C_i - R_i \right) \times A}{L_f \times h_f \times T}$$

Where T is the economic lifetime of the project in years, CF_t is the total cash flow of the project at time t, r is the discount rate, I is the total initial investment, C_i is the annual cost of the project, R_i is the annual revenue of the project, A is the discount factor (based on T and r), L_f is the full load capacity in kW and h_f is the project's annual full load equivalent operating hours.

For both key metrics, two scenarios were developed. The first scenario was without potential additional commercialization of the model, whereas the second scenario included additional potential revenues. However, both scenarios include revenues from cold storage rent, as this was the key revenue source for all models. Model-specific assumptions were discussed in the corresponding section.

Results

The study has two main objectives: (1) to determine whether the hybrid-cooling model is technically and economically feasible and (2) to address the potential scope for its implementation in rural off-grid areas where no grid connection is expected within the next 15 years. Results are presented in relation to each objective in turn.

Objective 1: Technical and economic feasibility

To satisfy these objectives, data was collected through focus group discussions (FGD) with farmers and traders and seven in-depth interviews (IDIs) with farmers. A traditional cold storage with a storage capacity of 15,000 MT, about 750 times bigger than the capacity of the potential solar-biomass hybrid cold storage for which we identify the potential scope, was visited in Rangpur. Interviews with other stakeholders of the cold storage were also conducted in Rangpur. In addition, a key informant interview (KII) was conducted with the Bangladesh Cold Storage Association (BCSA), who is responsible for coordination across all cold storage owners. Moreover, to satisfy our objective, findings from IDCOL Company, Bangladesh, who has experience of running some biomass-based renewable energy projects in Bangladesh, have also been presented in the paper.

Storage facility

According to The Energy and Resources Institute (TERI) in India, cold storage facilities in India are used for storing potatoes, which itself faces a problem. Since farmers have serious financial constraints and are typically in need of direct cash, they may not even store potatoes when prices are low but may sell immediately to market. Farmers in Bangladesh seem to be especially interested in storing potato seeds. Nowadays they mostly buy the seeds because they cannot store their own seeds effectively, but if they had the ability to store their own seeds, the farmers could reduce the investment required for their potato production.

Storage time

All stakeholder groups indicated that farmers and traders would typically store their potato seeds for nine to ten months of the year, but the time can vary depending on the farmer's or trader's needs. At the focus groups, the farmers indicated that typically potatoes are harvested from the beginning of November until the end of December.

Rental costs

It was evident that farmers were disadvantaged compared to the traders, as all stakeholder groups indicated that farmers paid a higher rental rate than traders for exactly the same level of service, since as smaller businesses they were in a weaker position to negotiate.

It was also revealed from this study that, regardless of the chosen length of storage time, rent is fixed. Whether it is kept for a month or the entire nine-month period, the same price needs to be paid when the produce is removed at the completion of the storage period. Additionally, it is worth mentioning that rent is paid on a "per sack"-basis.

Capacity and land requirements

According to the storage facility manager, the 15,000 MT cold storage has five chambers, each of which can store 35,000 sacks of potatoes, which would imply a total capacity of 175,000 sacks. However, the manager reported that the actual capacity of the facility was 147,000 sacks, somewhat less than suggested. Each sack weighs approximately 85 kilograms. The entire facility requires 3.25 acres of land to operate. One thousand one hundred boxes are kept in the front and back shade. The sacks of potatoes are stacked, one on top of the other, inside the storage and along the stairway leading to the top floor.

Objective 2: Potential scope for implementation in rural off-grid areas

From the focus groups and interviews it became clear that there are not enough cold storage facilities available in Rangpur to satisfy potential demand, even for potato crops alone. The farmers and traders indicated that they would prefer to have more availability of cold storage, and currently, only seed potatoes are kept in the cold storage. From these findings, it can be concluded that there is clearly a market to implement a cold storage facility in Rangpur. Three possible models were initially studied; Solar, Biomass and Solar/Biomass hybrid. Since the last was found to be most suitable, this is discussed below.

Solar-biomass hybrid cold storage model

There is a significant gap in existing research on solar-biomass hybrid cold storage, especially in the case of Bangladesh. However, there is some information on the solar-biomass hybrid project in India. The project is a joint partnership of TERI, THERMAX and NISE. Further research for the prospect of solar-biomass hybrid cold storage in the context of Bangladesh has also been done by visiting various organizations dealing with solar and biomass operations.

Solar-biomass cold storage in the context of India

The most relevant solar-biomass hybrid cold storage is located in India and is owned by TERI. This system is shown as Figure 3.1 below.[1]

TERI currently has a working hybrid cold storage plant in the center of a rural area in Gurgaon, India. The project was initiated in two phases, firstly to develop the technology and secondly to understand the social impact of implementation. The project has been running for two years now.

Economic features

It is reasonable to expect that the investment cost for installing a hybrid cold storage is significantly larger than for either a solar or a biomass-only cold storage, since the hybrid combines all the components of a biomass cooling model and those of a solar thermal model.

> Maintenance is relatively simple and the costs are low. Further operation costs are mainly related to the input of biomass.
>
> An expert from TERI during KII

At the time of research, the cost per unit of electricity was valued at INR 18, which is about USD 0.30, whereas the price of grid electricity in India is about INR 2–3 per unit (USD 0.03–0.05 approximately). Hence, the electricity generated is significantly more expensive than grid electricity. Since TERI and Thermax are still testing and adjusting the system, it can be improved further in terms of efficiency. This could result in decreased generation cost of per unit of electricity. As one of the respondents mentioned:

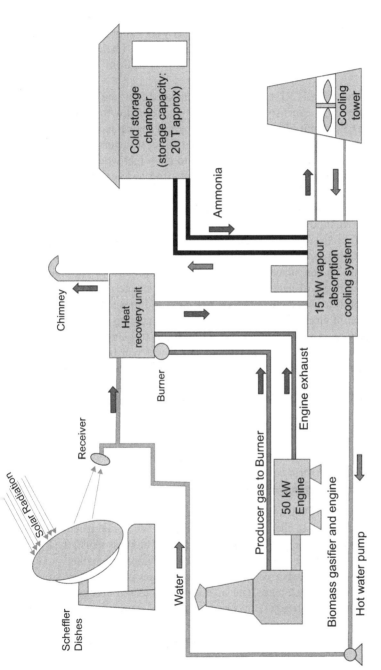

Figure 3.1 Graphic model of the solar-biomass hybrid cold storage system (TERI)

Narula & Mann, 2014

In order to sell electricity to the villagers and generate additional revenue, the relatively high-priced electricity should provide the villagers with sufficient economic benefits, which it does, I believe.

An expert from TERI during KII

As mentioned by TERI, the electricity generated from the hybrid model is three times more expensive than electricity generated with a diesel engine. It is USD 3 per unit of fuel wood for the hybrid engine and USD 1 per unit using diesel fuel. Feasibility also depends on local factors and size of the plant. For small plants, people are hired to chop fuel wood manually, but for larger plants it is more efficient and cost effective to use machines. Considering all the factors, operating costs for the biomass plant would be INR 10 per kg at least. Operating cost for only the fuel wood is very high, about INR 4 per kg if bought from the market. However, if the fuel wood is bought directly from the source, then the cost will be reduced to INR 2 per kg.

Information on revenue generation was also confidential. However, participants in the survey mentioned that if the hybrid model functions essentially like a tri-generation system, it can generate more revenue. Tri-generation refers to combining cooling, heat and power for simultaneous generation of electricity and useful heating and cooling from the combustion of a fuel or a solar heat collector. From this tri-generation system, the cooling will be used for cold storage, the power will be used for village electrification and the heat will be used for heating requirements in the surrounding villages. If these three sources are utilized efficiently, then it will be possible to generate revenue and make the hybrid model a success.

Discussion

Solar-biomass hybrid cold storage in the context of Bangladesh

In the context of Bangladesh, solar-biomass hybrid cold storage could add a new dimension to the cold storage solution. When compared with the two alternative models, which are solar alone or biomass alone, the hybrid cold storage will be able to mitigate each individual technology's (solar technology and biomass technology) disadvantages and the energy sources will complement each other. The solar unit will be used in bright sunshine, whereas during the foggy/rainy season, especially during the monsoon season (June–September), when sunlight is insufficient, biomass will be able to keep the system running. However, there needs to be enough biomass resources to ensure smooth operation of the system. For this, the hybrid plant needs to be implemented near the biomass resources. Also, because of availability issues, the biomass has to be rice husk rather than woody biomass, despite the fact that the latter has a higher combustion efficiency.

For solar PV use in electricity generation in rural Bangladesh for cold storage purpose, it is always a good idea to select those specific areas that have the highest sunlight irradiation. Solar thermal energy could play a role similar to solar PV, but there is not much research on this topic in Bangladesh. Which type of technology will be more suitable in the future is a matter for further research.

From the findings, it can be assumed that for a small scale (20 MT cold storage) any one of the three models could be chosen. In a hybrid model of solar and biomass energy, solar thermal energy is preferable to solar electric energy. This is due to the fact that heat from solar thermal energy can complement the heat generated by biomass gasification, to power the thermal cooling system. This optimizes the total efficiency of the system.

Village electrification is a crucial part of the hybrid model, since this will lead to the economic empowerment of the local villagers and add substantial value to the use of a hybrid model. The cost per unit of electricity is higher than the price paid for grid electricity. However, it was determined from our survey data results that when the villagers can benefit substantially from electricity and the national grid is not accessible, they will be willing to pay for it. Hybrid cold storage in Bangladesh can be economically feasible once the model is further commercialized and subsidies can be used to implement the cold storage units.

Conclusion

From the above discussion, all three models (solar, biomass and solar/biomass hybrid) can be feasible given that the feasibility parameters are chosen wisely. A cold storage unit with solar PV technology is more feasible than a cold storage based on solar thermal technology, due to the greater efficiency and availability of the PV technology in Bangladesh. When considering whether to install a solar cold storage unit, efficiency of the solar panels is an important factor to consider. The relatively low efficiency of contemporary solar panels results in a very strong downward pressure on the NPV. The project, which has a substantially negative NPV and limited options for revenue growth, is therefore very reliant on government or NGO subsidies. However, if either the cost of the panels decreased or the efficiency of the panels increased, there would be a strong positive impact on the economic feasibility of the solar PV cold storage. This could eventually lead to an LCOE that lies closer to the grid price of electricity.

The solar-biomass hybrid models are expected to have a significantly negative NPV, mainly due to the large investment costs. This implies that the economic feasibility will strongly rely on subsidies from governments or other organizations. Given the fact that India is already operating cold storages that are run by solar and biomass energy with the support of their government, it is assumed that this may be possible for the case of Bangladesh. This will require a larger investment outlay due to the additional components, but there are significant cost reduction opportunities once the model is standardized and commercialized. The long-term economic benefits for the farmers and local community are hard to value but are very relevant for the justification of the subsidies which would make the project feasible. If the model works out for the farmers and the local residents, the electricity received by them will open income-earning opportunities, enable children to study at home after dark and even allow women and girls to get involved in activities such as knitting/sewing, which they cannot do without proper electrification. Eventually these changes will lead to reduced poverty and improved livelihoods.

Note

1 *Source:* TERI (2012) *Solar-Biomass Hybrid Cold Storage-cum-Power Generation system for Rural Applications.* http://www.teriin.org/opinion/solar-biomass-hybrid-cold-storage-cum-power-generation-system-rural-applications

References

Bangladesh Rehabilitation Assistance Committee (BRAC), & SEFA. (2015). *International Development Project: An Exploration of Post-Harvest Perishable Food Loss in Bangladesh.* Dhaka. Retrieved from https://issuu.com/sefa_uva/docs/complete_idp_project_version_10

Egger, U. (n.d.). *Potato Processing in Bangladesh: The Rolling Stone, School of Agricultural, Forest and Food Sciences, Bern University of Applied Science* [Online]. Retrieved from www.katalyst.com.bd/docs/Potato%20case%20study.pdf [Accessed on 10 August 2014].

Food and Agriculture Organization (FAO). (2011). *Global Food Losses and Food Waste.* Food and Agriculture Organization of the United Nations, Germany.

Hassan, M. K., Chowdhury, B. L. D., & Akhter, N. (2010). *Post Harvest Loss Assessment: A Study to Formulate Policy for Loss Reduction of Fruits and Vegetables and Socioeconomic Uplift of the Stakeholders.* NFPCSP. Retrieved from www.nfpcsp.org/agridrupal/content/post-harvest-loss-assessment-study-formulate-policy-loss-reduction-fruits-and-vegetables-and

Hossain, M., & Miah, M. (2009). *Post Harvest Losses and Technical Efficiency of Potato Storage Systems in Bangladesh* (Rep.). Bangladesh Agricultural Research Institute.

Narula, A., & Mann, L. (2014). *Arrived Cold Storage Solution for Villages: Akshay Urja* [Online]. *7*(5), 10–15. https://mnre.gov.in/file-manager/akshay-urja/march-april-2014/EN/10-15.pdf [Accessed on 10 August 2014].

United Nations Development Programme (UNDP). (2017). *Sustainable Development Goals*. United Nations Development Programme [Online]. Retrieved from www.undp.org/content/undp/en/home/sustainable-development-goals/goal-7-affordable-and-clean-energy.html [Accessed on 12 February 2017].

World Bank (WB). (2014). *Lighting Up Rural Communities in Bangladesh*. Washington, DC: World Bank Group.

Part 4

Sustainable Development Goal 13

Climate action

4 Discerning the mayhem

Negotiating climate change and sustainable development

Sharmi Palit

Introduction

In 2014, the *Times of India* daily newspaper (Raheja, 2014) reported that a study conducted by the World Health Organization "ranks India amongst the world's worst for its polluted air". The study identified 20 of the world's worst affected cities, 13 lying within India itself, including Delhi, Patna, Ahmedabad, Lucknow, Amritsar and others (India TV, 2015). Subsequently, the international non-governmental organization Greenpeace (2017) reported that the air pollution crisis in India was a "national problem" that killed 1.2 million Indians every year, and affected 3% of the GDP.

Today, not only India but also the entire global community is struggling with the unmitigated consequences of its ambitious but inconsiderate developmental past. Unplanned industrialization and extreme exploitation of natural resources have resulted in environmental disasters such as cyclones and famine attaining persistent space in our everyday lives. As a result, in 2015 the United Nations (United Nations Development Programme [UNDP], n.d.) developed the Agenda for United Nations Sustainable Development Goals (SDG) 2030, where more than one goal was dedicated to issues of pollution, climate change and global warming. Consequently, the study in this paper was conducted under the broad theme of United Nations Sustainable Development Goal (SDG) 13 on climate action, which calls for immediate actions to be undertaken at the local, national and global level to avoid the "irreplaceable" consequences of nature (*ibid*), and SDG 3 on "good health and well-being for people".

This study considers the pollution crisis in the city of New Delhi, India. Based on the perspectives of the youth, it is argued that there is an urgent imperative to include sociology in the current discourse on climate change, global warming and sustainable development. This is because to discuss degrading environmental conditions and the consequent need for concrete solutions, yet to exclude the vast majority of human population from the dialogue, is a major shortcoming. I argue that this lack of inclusion of the people has led to a widening gap between society and policymaking in India and elsewhere. It is only when we make efforts to bridge this gap and include larger sections of society that we can collectively and successfully confront the problem of extreme climatic conditions and pollution.

The study conducted in this paper had three research objectives:

1   To explore how the youth understand air pollution and climate change.
2   To establish the views of the youth on potential climate change mitigation, both at the micro and the macro level.
3   To explore the odd even policy that was implemented to curb the air pollution crises in New Delhi, India.

Research methodology

This is a preliminary qualitative study based on the perspectives of youth, namely the students of Jawaharlal Nehru University (JNU), regarding air pollution in New Delhi, India. JNU was chosen because as a premier Indian academic institution it included a diverse student body that varied across social class, regional and religious identity and disciplinary standpoints. As a pilot study, the sample size was limited to 100 respondents who were selected on the basis of stratified and snowball sampling techniques. The method of data collection was unstructured interviews.

The city of New Delhi has had a long struggle with air pollution. Even ‑a cursory glance at public records and newspaper articles reveals how the mortality of Delhi citizens has been affected by air pollution. The smog, a deadly mixture of particulate matter, fog and noxious gases from vehicular emissions, non-sustainable agricultural practices (like slash and burn) and industrial and construction activities has prevailed in the city on many occasions in recent times, ringing alarms bells and prompting a breakthrough in people's rather stoic indifference.

With regards to the definition of the term "youth", despite the commonly accepted definition (United Nations Educational, Scientific and Cultural Organization [UNESCO], n.d.) referring to all individuals between 15 and 24 years of age, the operational definition in this paper was extended to include individuals between 18 and 29 years of age. This was done for two reasons: Firstly, the Indian government (Ministry of Youth Affairs and Sports, Government of India, 2014) recognizes "youth" as individuals between 15 and 29 years of age. Secondly, as a higher-level academic institution, the students were all above 18 years of age, with the majority pursuing either postgraduate or doctoral courses. Thus, it seemed logical to modify the limits of age categorization of youth to from 15–24 years to 18–20 years.

Results and discussion

The interviews with the respondents began with a simple thought experiment: what is the first thought or image that comes to your mind when "Delhi" and "climate" are said together? The responses produced words such as "smog", "poison", "horrible", "harsh", "gas chamber", "pollution", "black" and related vocabulary. The responses to this question set the tone of the conversation that followed. Although opinions varied on the veracity of human-induced climate change and global warming, there was a complete consensus regarding the air pollution crisis in the city. Unlike the subtler immediate effects of climate change, in the recent past, the city's inhabitants have had to confront the inescapable effects of poor air quality in their daily lives. It was of interest to establish whether the respondents could make a connection between the air pollution in the city and the larger issues of climate change and global warming. The interviews that were conducted revolved around three major themes: the role of culture, government and youth.

Climate change and youth: perspectives

The interviews began with the basic question: *what do you understand by climate change and global warming?* Since increasing attention is being paid to climate change and global warming in the media and in everyday conversations, most respondents were generally able to articulate some standard definition, relating to the increasing average temperature of the Earth's surface. Prompted further, most cited examples of melting glaciers, rising sea level and enhanced famines. Thus, it was safe to state that the respondents had at least a layperson's understanding of the problem. However, there exists a more scientific explanation of the problem that was given by a professor from the School of Environmental Science (SES), JNU. Simply stated, he suggested that New Delhi itself did not directly contribute to changing global climatic conditions, but rather put an immense amount of stress on factors that contributed towards it. These factors included biomass burning, thermal power plants, vehicular emissions and surface dust.

Consequently, in relation to the first theme on the role of culture, most respondents agreed that the unique culture of the city played a central role in the present pollution crises. Recognizing Tylor's (1871) characterization of "culture", most respondents blamed it for the deplorable conditions of the city environment and high levels of air pollution. Acquisition and ownership of material goods, or in Veblen's (1965) terminology "goods for conspicuous consumption", were widely cited as being both symbolic of belonging to a particular social class, and also a means to attaining upward social mobility. Within this rationale, there was overwhelming emphasis on acquiring more and more material goods, and acting in ways that would otherwise be unnecessary. For instance, a respondent cited the example of the emerging tuition culture in the city. Regardless of whether a student required the extra help from tuition classes, parents tended to enrol their children in these classes. This was often done to establish that their child did not lag behind in the competition and had access to some exclusive tuition class, regardless of the fees.

Regarding the role of government, a majority agreed that the government had indeed undertaken various steps to combat the pollution level. However, disagreements emerged when the young people were asked about the credibility of those actions. One group argued that the attempts were half-hearted, with no visible successful results in either the short or long run. They believed that the government had particularly failed to ensure strict vigilance over the actions and policies that they had introduced. On the other hand, other students believed that the blame could not be put entirely on the government; unless people actually supported the authorities, all attempts to secure results would be rendered futile.

Finally, in relation to the specific potential of young people to act, not all respondents agreed on the appropriate role and function. Omitting those who were entirely unsure about the youth role, there were two main groups of responses. The first group believed that youth would or could be the leaders and primary driving agents of the movement to secure change and mitigate the air pollution. The second group believed that society comprised of people of all age groups, hence the responsibility had to be shared by all, not only resting with young people.

Solutions: the micro and the macro level

A section of the interviews was dedicated to the solutions that the youth believed could possibly mitigate the pollution crises in the city, as well as make the population as a whole more sensitive to the changing climatic conditions of the city, nation and world. Consequently, the solutions offered could be broadly classified into two categories – micro- and macro-level solutions.

Micro-level solutions

Micro-level solutions essentially referred to steps that need to be undertaken at the level of individual actors, directed at their beliefs and practices. In the long run, respondents felt that changes introduced at the micro level would have a lasting and wider impact since they brought alterations in everyday routine choices. Thus, if people were motivated to be more ecologically sensitive and conscious of their daily practices, then not only would pressure over natural resources and pollution levels be greatly reduced, but also factors triggering changing climatic patterns and global warming would be lowered.

Consequently, the first step would be to alter our process of socialization, which is the process through which an individual internalizes the cultural goals and normative standards of his or her society (Parsons et al., 1956). If from the onset we socialize our children to be environmentally sensitive, then the probability of our callous attitude and resulting actions towards the natural world being repeated would be highly unlikely. Respondents suggested that it was important to understand that the responsibility for socialization rested equally with the education system as with family and kinship networks.

Secondly, in order to alter the socialization process, our socio-cultural practices need to be first addressed and changed. For instance, the undue importance that is attributed to symbolic aspects of our material culture such as on luxury cars or air-conditioners has to be forgone. As explained by Marcuse (1964), such growing demands for consumerism, along with the superfluous emphasis placed on mass culture, make us "one dimensional" in terms of our thoughts and activities, leaving us bereft of our rationality and creative faculties. Not only does this take a further toll on the steadily depleting natural resources, but it also obstructs our vision and prevents us from considering the consequences of our actions, especially for the environment.

Finally, another method to make changes at the micro level would be to encourage innovative practices that would replace the existing mainstream non-eco-friendly lifestyle. This again is intrinsically linked to the previous solutions and examples of innovative practices including rewarding (not simply monetarily) tree plantations, waste management and recycling, encouraging walking and cycling and similar initiatives.

Macro-level solutions

Macro-level solutions referred to steps that respondents believed should be taken on a large scale, taking into account the entire city and directing changes at the societal level. Firstly, change through formal education was seen as critical. Education is a powerful tool that could be used to raise awareness about changing realities, not just of the city, but also of the entire nation and the world. This could be done by making changes in academic curricula and bringing students closer to the natural world. However, a few respondents also believed that "education" should not only be seen in terms of formal education certified by schools. Instead they felt that attempts should be made to "educate" the masses as well through means of awareness programmes and campaigns.

Secondly, most respondents believed that the government had to play a stronger role, both in terms of policy intervention and ensuring its implementation. A few recalled the failure of the government to enforce some of its earlier environmental actions such as the plastic ban, and drew parallels, primarily due to lack of strict vigilance and appropriate regulations. Thirdly, respondents suggested that the government should immediately shut down the active industries in and around the city and move them to surrounding tier two cities, that is, small towns and cities with a population ranging from 50,000 to 99,999 individuals (RBI, 2015). Such cities would not only welcome employment opportunities but would also help reduce the extreme population pressure of the capital. Next, it was thought that the state should take stricter actions to reduce vehicular emissions. This could include restricting the number of vehicles per household, introducing a carbon tax on vehicles and similar actions.

Furthermore, it was thought to be crucial that both the state and central government should promote and fund research to curb pollution levels in the city and country. A respondent from the School of Computational and Integrative Sciences, JNU cited an example from Mexico, wherein a novel concept of vertical gardens was introduced that involved growing plants on columns of flyovers, street dividers, etc. This was done through a scientific procedure, such that the plants did not harm the underlying concrete structures and absorbed harmful pollutants from the air and released oxygen. Finally, a few respondents thought that, if needed, the government could develop partnerships with private stakeholders and form public private partnerships (PPP). They believed that shared responsibility through joint ventures with private stakeholders could enable the government to implement schemes and raise awareness through campaigns, etc. more successfully and also ensure that the private partners would themselves be conscious of their actions in their respective ventures.

The case study: the odd even policy

The Delhi Government implemented the odd even policy on a trial basis from January 1–15, 2016 to curb air pollution in the city. It involved placing restrictions on private vehicles in the city on the basis of the last digit on their number plates. Within an operating time frame from 8 a.m. to 8 p.m., the policy mandated that on odd dates only cars with number plates ending with an odd digit would be allowed to move, whereas on even dates those ending with even digits would be allowed to move. Two wheelers and cars driven by women were exempt from this restriction. In addition, all construction activities were stopped, and diesel trucks and all vehicles older than 10 years were banned during this period. After the implementation period, the government declared the policy to be a success based on two reasons – a decrease in the number of vehicles on the road and comparatively lower levels of particulate matter (PM) in the air (Greenstone *et al.*, 2016). Based on this rationale, the government implemented the policy for a second time from April 15–30, 2016 (The Hindu, 2016). Thereafter, due to the appeal made by the Ministry of Environment, the Supreme Court passed a law that enabled a "Graded Response Action Plan" (GRAP) to come into force whenever the levels of particular matter (PM) in the air exceeded acceptable limits, i.e., when PM 2.5 crossed 300 $\mu g/m^3$ and PM 10 crossed the 500 $\mu g/m^3$ limit. The GRAP also included a temporary shutdown of various industries located in the city, and a prohibition of running of heavy and similar vehicles (Indian Express, 2017).

Although the policy was implemented only after careful study, the arbitrary declaration of its "success" by the government appears to be problematic. First and foremost, there were no third-party agencies or organizations that conducted an analysis on the impact of the policy: the declaration of success was a self-appraisal made by the government. Moreover, if "success" implies only a reduction in number of vehicles or PM levels in the air for that particular period, then the policy could be seen as a success. However, if "success" implies a breakthrough in people's perception towards decreasing air pollution by altering certain lifestyle choices, then it appears that the policy failed by a large extent. Secondly, to meet the high demands during the period, schools were shut down and buses were borrowed for public transportation. This is clearly not feasible in the long run as schools cannot be closed every time. Major logistical concerns, especially in terms of availability of adequate public transport, need to be tackled before the policy is implemented for the long term. Finally, the government implemented the policy from a top-down approach that did not take into account the rationale, preferences and impact of the section of society most affected. This is why the current study, through a sociological lens, attempts to assess the perspectives of the youth in order to conduct a bottom-up analysis of the policy. The twin parameters of social class and government policies were used in the analysis.

To begin, a majority of the respondents agreed that immediate steps had to be undertaken to mitigate the pollution crisis in the city. As far as this particular policy was concerned, there were mixed responses on the results of the odd even policy and not everyone agreed that it was a success. While some saw it as a success, others were more critical of the shortcomings like the exemption of two wheelers from being included. They also showed considerable skepticism towards the authenticity of the self-analysis made by the government. Some respondents said they were unaffected by the policy as they either did not live in the city or chose not to leave campus during that period. When questioned about the problems faced in everyday lives, responses ranged from not being overtly affected as public transport was their usual means of mobility to grateful for the reduced congestion to dissatisfaction over the lack of adequate public transport to cope with the sudden pressure. It is interesting to note that those who were generally satisfied with the policy often applauded it for reasons such as reductions in transit time, and less for reducing air pollution levels in the city.

Examining the policy from the standpoint of governmental policies, it has to be conceded that the government had undertaken various measures to bring attention to the problem, by raising awareness in campaigns, advertisements, radio announcements and newspapers. However, despite all efforts, no concrete long-term solutions emerged. Once the policy period was over, the number of private vehicles on the road rose again. Moreover, before the introduction of such policies the government needs to be realistic about the ability to cope with the changing demands of its services. One cannot expect the public to rely on public transport if adequate numbers of buses or metros are not available.

With regards to social class, during interviews it emerged that a considerable percentage of the respondents (broadly divided into two groups) believed that the policy had a differential impact on different sections of society. The first group felt that wealthier residents remained unaffected as they usually found means to evade the policy. One respondent said she had heard of cases wherein people exchanged cars amongst themselves (on the basis of the last digit of the number plates) or even bought or made alternative number plates for their cars, while another shared how a few of his acquaintances found it easier to pay the fine rather than confront the heavy rush in public transportation. In contrast, the second group believed that the urban poor remained unaffected by such policies. Habituated to rely completely on public transport, walking or cycling, this policy in particular hardly disrupted their lives. Instead, they found the upper strata of society, who relied heavily on private vehicles, to feel the heat much more intensely.

Consequently, the most crucial finding that emerged through this analysis pertains to the moral dilemmas between climate change and social justice. Firstly, it points towards the imbalance between those who contribute most towards air pollution and those who are the most affected by it. Although, regardless of all parameters of social stratification, the effects of air pollution and climate change impact all equally, yet one cannot brush aside the fact that the upper echelons of society are better able to confront these consequences. Thus, access to better health care facilities, affordability of innovative technological products like air purifiers, etc. enable them to escape the immediate impact of smog on their mortality. In sharp contrast, the lower classes not only are persistently subjected to the hazardous air, but also lack the monetary means to attain high quality goods and services to protect their health and well-being. Secondly, the analysis also highlights the reluctance of the elites towards altering certain lifestyle choices and acknowledging the responsibility and consequences of their actions. A tendency to escape the consequences by means of monetary power and loopholes in government policies becomes clearly visible.

To conclude, despite the differing viewpoints of Jawaharlal Nehru University students, an examination via a bottom-up approach suggests that the policy was not successful and, in fact, was entangled in a number of shortcomings. These include lack of central logistical preparations in relation to public transport and failure to make citizens understand the overall need to reduce acute air pollution because of its health implications. This then leads us to the argument made earlier regarding the need for changes to be made at the micro level to make citizens understand why actions must be taken to curb pollution levels immediately as bridging the gap between society and policymaking.

Conclusion

In conclusion, the current paper was an attempt to study the air pollution crises in the city of New Delhi, India through a sociological lens. Based on the perspectives of the youth, the paper discussed their perceptions regarding air pollution and climate change as well as the plausible solutions that could successfully mitigate the crises. In the latter half, a bottoms-up approach was used to conduct an analysis of the odd even policy implemented in the city. Despite it being a preliminary study, I hope to have established the need for a sociological discourse in global discussions of climate change, global warming and sustainable development. As illustrated in the paper, it becomes apparent that unless we include the larger sections of society and conceptualize a people-based approach to policymaking, issues of environmental degradation, pollution and climate change will never successfully be mitigated in the long run. As illustrated in the case of the odd even policy, until and unless we make a breakthrough in societal perceptions towards pollution, environmental degradation and climate change no real change can be made at the micro level that significantly influences individual beliefs and socio-cultural practices in our everyday lives.

Acknowledgements

I would like to thank Professor Amrita Sastry, Jesus and Mary College, University of Delhi for giving her invaluable input and support during the course of writing this paper.

References

Greenpeace. (2017). *Airpocalypse: Assessment of Air Pollution in Indian Cities.* Retrieved from www.greenpeace.org/india/Global/india/Airpoclypse-Not-just-Delhi-Air-in-most-Indian-cities-hazardous-Greenpeace-report.pdf

Greenstone, M., Harish, S., Sudarshan, A., & Pande, R. (2016). Yes, Delhi, it worked. *The Indian Express.* Retrieved from http://indianexpress.com/article/opinion/columns/odd-even-policy-delhi-pollution-yes-delhi-it-worked/

India TV. (2015, December 4). 13 of the 20 most polluted cities are in India. *India TV.* Retrieved from www.indiatvnews.com/news/india/13-out-of-20-most-polluted-cities-in-world-are-from-india-54104.html

Indian Express. (2017, January 17). Govt. notifies plan: Odd even, car curbs depending on SPM count. *The Indian Express.* Retrieved from http://indianexpress.com/article/india/govt-notifies-plan-odd-even-car-curbs-depending-on-spm-count-4477714/

Marcuse, H. (1964). *One-Dimensional Man: The Ideology of Advanced Industrial Society.* London: Sphere Books.

Ministry of Youth Affairs and Sports. (2014). *National Youth Policy 2014.* Government of India. Retrieved from www.rgniyd.gov.in/sites/default/files/pdfs/scheme/nyp_2014.pdf

Parsons, T., Bales, R. F., & Olds, J. (1956). *Family Socialization and Interaction Process* (Vol. 7). Great Britain: Routledge.

Raheja, V. (2014, May 9). India ranks amongst the world's worst for its polluted air. *The Times of India.* Retrieved from http://timesofindia.indiatimes.com/home/environment/pollution/India-ranks-among-theworlds-worst-for-its-polluted-air-WHO/articleshow/34890249.cms

RBI (Reserve Bank of India). (2015). *Details of Tier-Wise Classification of Centers Based on Population.* (Annex. 4). Retrieved from https://rbi.org.in/scripts/NotificationUser.aspx?Id=9817&Mode=0#an4

Staff Reporter (2016, April 15) Odd Even Rule comes back to Delhi from April 15. *The Hindu.* Retrieved from: http://www.thehindu.com/news/cities/Delhi/Odd-even-rule-comes-back-to-Delhi- from-April-15/article14073650.ece

Tylor, E. B. (1871). *Primitive Culture* (Vol. 1). New York: J. P. Putnam's Sons.

United Nations Development Programme. (n.d.). *Sustainable Development Goals.* Retrieved from www.undp.org/content/undp/en/home/sustainable-development-goals.html

United Nations Educational, Scientific and Cultural Organization. (n.d.). *What Do We Mean by "Youth"?* Retrieved from www.unesco.org/new/en/social-and-human-sciences/themes/youth/youth-definition/

Veblen, T. (1965). *The Theory of the Leisure Class: 1899.* New York: A. M. Kelley, Bookseller.

5 Assessment of the climate change-induced vulnerabilities of coastal regions and adaptation practices of arable agriculture in Bangladesh

Sabrina Zaman, Mohammad Sujauddin and Nazmul Ahsan Khan

Introduction

Climate change is a genuine threat to the world community in the twenty-first century. The global climate is changing at an increasing rate compared to the natural background, and it is widely accepted that this will intensify natural hazards such as floods, cyclones or hurricanes, sea level rise, soil salinity and other key elements of the Earth's human support systems (Intergovernmental Panel on Climate Change [IPCC], 2007, 2001). The global average surface temperature has increased over the twentieth century by about 0.6±0.2°C (IPCC, 2001), with a notable increase being recorded late in the century, and the rate of change appears to be escalating. It is estimated that the frequency of extreme low temperatures has reduced while the frequency of extreme high temperatures has slightly increased (IPCC, 2001), and that this pattern will continue unless major changes are made to lifestyles and particularly the emissions of greenhouse gases such as carbon dioxide and methane. Whilst climate change is a global phenomenon having widespread damaging impacts, low-lying, densely populated developing countries are particularly climate-sensitive. Bangladesh is likely to be one of the worst victims of future changes due to the direct impact of climate extremes on its economy and people. The low-lying coastal zone is vulnerable to multiple hazards such as sea level rise (Sarwar & Islam, 2013; Ali, 2000; Chowdhury *et al.*,1997), shoreline erosion and river sedimentation (Sarwar & Islam, 2013; Mikhailov & Dotsenko, 2007; Allison, 1998), flooding (Alauddin & Rahman, 2013; Sarwar & Islam, 2013; Islam & Sado, 2000), cyclones (Alauddin & Rahman, 2013; Alam *et al.*, 2003) and rising levels of soil and aquifer salinity (Alauddin & Rahman, 2013; Chowdhury & Karim, 1998). Sea level rise – the combined effect of thermal expansion due to ocean warming and melting of land-based ice, i.e., glaciers and ice sheets – and cyclones have the deadliest impacts on the agricultural sector along the coast of Bangladesh. Arable cultivation, which makes up over half of the agricultural sector (56%), contributes about 22% of the total GNP and supports about two thirds (65%) of the labor force of Bangladesh (Nishat & Mukherjee, 2013), is potentially seriously affected.

There is a considerable body of research on climate change vulnerabilities (Islam *et al.*, 2015; Nishat & Mukherjee, 2013; Sarwar & Islam, 2013), but literature covering adaptive practices in the arable sector is scattered and patchy in coverage (Saha *et al.*, 2016; Sutradhar *et al.*, 2015; Alauddin & Rahman, 2013). This paper reviews the vulnerabilities of arable agriculture to sea level rise and cyclones while outlining all of the known adaptation practices undertaken by Bangladeshi farmers in these coastal areas. The intention is to fill the knowledge gap on adaptive practices for crop production, and to provide a base for further research, innovation and scaling up of those approaches. This will bring the region closer to achieving United Nations Sustainable Development Goal 2, on ending hunger, achieving food security and improved nutrition and promoting sustainable agriculture, and Goal 13, on taking urgent action to combat climate change and its impacts.

Methods

An extensive and detailed literature search was undertaken by using the popular internet search engines Google and Google Scholar, seeking literature classified with any of the keywords or titles associated with 'coastal region of Bangladesh', 'climate change', 'climate change impacts', 'vulnerabilities', 'agriculture' and 'adaptation'. This was followed by using OARE and My Athens to access peer-reviewed journals. Bibliographies from the primary recognized literature related to the topic, and the websites of related national and international organizations, were also drawn upon to generate further material. We selected 114 literatures in total relevant to vulnerabilities of climate change and adaptation practices of arable agriculture of coastal Bangladesh, which included both peer-reviewed and non-peer-reviewed journals; open access journals; government reports; non-governmental, charity and international organizations' publications; conference proceedings; book chapters; academic dissertations; and other 'grey' literature.

The identified literature was classified by virtue of its potential relationship to assisting the development of future scenarios, vulnerabilities and impacts regarding climate change and adaptation practices in the coastal regions of Bangladesh. The first cluster of publications included those presenting the historical basis and evidence for climate change, based on analysis of current and future estimated trends. The second type of publications included those describing the adaptation needs of Bangladesh as a whole, and the potential of those adaptations to reduce vulnerabilities, as the country attempts to ensure its own food security in a world affected by climate change. The third group included publications presenting case studies on vulnerability and adaptation approaches in coastal areas.

Vulnerabilities and adaptation to arable agriculture in the coastal regions of Bangladesh

Climatic vulnerability of Bangladesh

The impacts of climate change are not evenly distributed across the world. The developing and less developed countries of Asia and Africa are highly susceptible to climate change as a result of their weak economic structure, institutional frailties, and high dependency on climate-sensitive natural resources. Bangladesh, an agriculturally based developing country, is particularly vulnerable to climate change (Hossain, 2013; IPCC, 2007) because of its geographical location on the Bay of Bengal and at the mouth of major seasonally flooding river systems, its high population density, poor socio-economic conditions and considerable dependency on agriculture and fisheries (Rahman, 2011). Moreover, according to Rahman there is still a general absence of awareness and insufficiently resourced institutional support to cope with and plan for these vulnerabilities.

The annually published Germanwatch 'Global Climate Risk Index' (GCRI) analyses to what extent countries across the world have been affected by the impacts of weather-related loss events (storms, floods, heat waves and so on.) in terms of economic losses and mortality. The most recent data available, mainly from 2015, are considered in the latest report, when the countries affected most in 2015 were Mozambique, Dominica and Malawi. For the whole period from 1996 to 2015 Honduras, Myanmar and Haiti were the worst affected. The GCRI identified Honduras, Myanmar and Haiti as the most affected countries in 2016, but in the last 20 years from 1995 to 2016 Bangladesh has appeared in sixth position, largely as a result of climate changes that are already apparent. This is an increasingly dangerous situation.

Major vulnerabilities of the coastal region

Among the different climatic stressors mentioned previously, sea level rise and cyclones have the most serious implications for coastal crop agriculture. Islam and Peterson (2009) examined tropical cyclones in the coastal regions for about 127 years, for the period of 1877–2003, which revealed pre-monsoon (May–June) and post-monsoon (October–November) as the peak seasons for cyclones, including 70% of total tropical cyclones, and showed an increasing trend over the period.

The coastal region of Bangladesh will also face serious consequences from sea level rise because of its low elevation and topography. Rahman (2011) noted that a World Bank study presented the implications of 10 cm, 25 cm and 1 m rises in sea level by 2020, 2050 and 2100, respectively, and estimated that it will affect 2%, 4% and 17.5% of total land mass in Bangladesh subsequently. A study by the SAARC Meteorological Research Council observing 22 years of tidal data from three coastal stations suggested that the sea level is typically rising by between about 4 and 8 mm per year along the coast of Bangladesh, most rapidly in the eastern areas around Cox's Bazar (Table 5.1) (Hossain, 2013; Sarwar & Islam, 2013; Rahman, 2011; Ministry of Environment & Forest [MoEF], 2005). However, even a 4 mm annual rise has the potential to create major challenges over decades, when the configuration of the coastline is so low.

Vulnerability of crop agriculture to cyclones and sea level rise

Arable agriculture, one of the dominant sectors of Bangladesh economy, is potentially severely affected by climatic change-induced shifts in typical circumstances, and to intermittent extremes. Agriculture contributes about 22% of the total GNP and supports about two-thirds (65%) of the labor force (Nishat & Mukherjee, 2013). Particular arable crops are reliant on specific climatic characteristics such as average temperatures and temperature ranges, precipitation totals and monthly distributions and relative humidity, and as a sector Bangladeshi arable agriculture is likely to be more vulnerable to changes in conditions than fisheries, livestock rearing, human health or the availability of drinking water will be. Table 5.2 shows the pattern, and aggregate scoring of different types of climate stressors for the various sectors, based on the methodologies of Hossain (2013) and MoEF (2005). Across the board, extreme high temperatures are the most threatening of the likely climatic changes, but cyclones and saline intrusion are of particular

Table 5.1 Tidal trends in three coastal monitoring stations

Tidal Station	Region	Trend (mm per year)
Hiron Point	Western	4.0
Char Changa	Central	6.0
Cox's Bazar	Eastern	7.8

Source: Hossain (2013); MoEF (2005); Rahman (2011); Sarwar and Islam (2013)

Table 5.2 Intensity of impacts of climate change on different sectors in Bangladesh

| Vulnerable sectors | Physical vulnerability context (climate change and climatic events) | | | | | | | | Vulnerability score |
| | Extreme temperature | Drought | Flood | | Cyclone & storm surges | Sea level rise | | Soil erosion | |
			Riverine flood	Flash flood		Coastal inundation	Salinity intrusion		
Arable agriculture	3	3	1	2	3	2	3	0	17
Fisheries	2	2	2	1	1	1	1	0	10
Livestock	2	0	0	1	3	2	3	0	11
Infrastructure	1	0	2	1	1	2	0	3	10
Industries	2	0	2	1	1	3	2	0	11
Biodiversity	2	0	2	0	1	3	3	0	11
Health	3	0	2	0	2	1	3	0	11
Human health	0	0	0	0	3	0	0	3	6
Energy	2	0	1	0	1	1	0	0	5

Source: Adopted from MOEF (2005)

Notes: 0 = not vulnerable, 1 = slightly vulnerable, 2 = moderately vulnerable, 3 = seriously vulnerable significance for crop production. Livestock rearing is also one of the more seriously affected sectors.

Recurrent tropical cyclones with their associated storm surges are one of the main dangers to coastal agriculture (Hossain, 2013). Cyclones affect coastal land in two ways. Firstly, standing crops and trees can be completely destroyed by the combination of sudden high velocity winds, and water temporarily flooding across normally dry ground, tearing growing vegetation from its roots. Secondly, the longer-term impacts of cyclones are associated with storm surges whose massive waves can grow to over nine metres in height as they track northwards across the sea-land interface (Khalil, 1993, cited in Sarwar & Islam, 2013), bringing saline water across coastal lands and causing soil salinization. Formerly productive agricultural lands are turned into unproductive fields that can take years to recover from the addition of marine salts (Sarwar & Islam, 2013).

FAO/ GIEWS Global Watch (2007) reported that according to the Department of Agricultural Extension of Bangladesh, the loss in 'Aman' rice (paddy rice generally sown by broadcasting, and transplanted between December and January) during the devastating tropical Cyclone Sidr in November 2007 amounted to 1.23 million tons, with 535,707 tons in the four severely affected districts, 555,997 tons in nine badly affected districts and 203,600 tons in a further 17 moderately affected districts of Bangladesh. Cyclone Sidr also caused a semi-permanent reduction in the rice cultivation area as well as reduced the rice harvest (Anik et al., 2012), and caused several thousand deaths. Winds of over 250 km per hour were recorded, and a coastal surge of between five and six metres occurred, forcing sea water up through river channels and creeks, and drowning land areas; some 2 million people were successfully evacuated, but soil salinization in the Sundarbans mangroves and adjacent areas was expected to persist for up to 40 years. Similarly, following the less serious Cyclone Aila in May 2009, long-term water logging with saline water occurred for over two years in some parts of the coastal area. The table below (Table 5.3) shows the crop land damaged by a 1991 cyclone, and more recent Cyclones Sidr and Aila (Sarwar & Islam, 2013).

Sea level rise will affect agriculture and more specifically food production (Shamsuddoha & Chowdhury, 2007). Sea level rise disturbs agriculture in three ways: through saline intrusion into aquifers at different depths, by direct surface flooding of low ground and by increasing the complexity of damage in conjunction with cyclones. Agricultural production in the coastal region can be affected by the combined effects of all three (Anik *et al.*, 2012). The use of increasingly brackish groundwater and surface water derived from formerly fresh streams for agricultural purposes such

Table 5.3 Coastal crop lands damaged by major cyclones

Sector	Damage Type	1991 Cyclone	Cyclone SIDR (2007)	Cyclone Aila (2009)
Crop Land	Fully	47,673	120,000	31,357
	Partially	320,494	1390,000	99,540

Source: Adopted from Sarwar and Islam (2013)

as irrigation also degrades the soil further, and decreases the production of crops that cannot tolerate salt (Islam *et al.*, 2015; Sarwar, 2005; MoEF, 2005). The increased numbers of salt water shrimp farms in the Bangladesh coastal region also suggests increased salinity in formerly fresh creeks and streams (Iftekhar & Islam, 2004).

Adaptation practices in the crop agricultural sector

Agriculture in the coastal region has for some years been adopting various climate change adaptation practices, including hard engineering measures, softer socio-economic measures and technological innovations, to cope with the existing and increasing climatic pressures (Saha *et al.*, 2016). The exposed coastal districts are experiencing more adaptation actions than the interior district, and notably, among the exposed districts, Khulna, Satkhira, Bhola, Bagerhat, Pirojpur and Barguna have been experiencing more adaptation measures than the rest. Khulna and Satkhira faced the maximum number of adaptations of about 9.8% of the total amount of adaptations, where Bholla, Bagerhat, Pirojpur, Barguna and Jessore faced 6.7%, 6.5%, 6.2%, 6.2% and 6.0% of the total adaptations respectively (Saha *et al.*, 2016).

So far, relatively few research studies have captured the existing adaptation practices of coastal farmers. In an exceptional recent study, Saha *et al.* (2016) found that of the different potential agricultural adaptation practices associated with climate change, 28% were found to be associated with the use of new crops or crop varieties, for instance, salt- and submergence-tolerant rice and other cereal varieties, short-duration vegetables and pulses and the introduction of cash crops such as sunflowers, watermelon and sesame. The remainder included a wide variety of activities and shifts in behavior. Drawing together the remainder of the literature enables an overview of the prevailing adaptation practices in the agricultural sector in the coastal region of Bangladesh (Table 5.4), filling the research gap and providing a base for future research on this sector.

Table 5.4 Adaptive/modified agricultural methods practiced in the coastal region of Bangladesh

Adaptation method	Areas	Suitable Crops/ Crops Cultivated	Climatic effect
Raised bed[3, 5]	Coastal saline zone and drought-prone areas[4], Noakhali and Shakira[5]	Watermelon, Okra, BARI Tomato -3	Water logging
Mulching[4]	Coastal saline zone and drought-prone areas[4]		
Water storage in crop fields[4]	Coastal lands and drought-prone areas[4]		
Ditch and dike method[1, 4]/ Sorjan system[2, 5]	Coastal saline-prone areas[4], Patuakhali[5]	Crops and fish[4], vegetables, i.e., lady's finger, chichinga, pumpkin, water gourd, bitter gourd, brinjal[1] and monsoon rice with fish or duck[5]	Salinity
Mound plantation[4]	Coastal saline affected areas[4]		
Zero tillage[1, 2, 5]	Drought-prone areas, flood-prone areas, saline-prone areas[1]	Potato, maize[1]	
Homestead gardening[2, 5, 6]		Leafy vegetables, i.e., kangkong, batisak, sweet testing stem, amaranth vegetable seedlings[1]	
Floating bed[2, 3, 4, 5]	Coastal areas	Vegetables, i.e., lady's finger, cucumber, bitter gourd, kohlrabi, pumpkin, water gourd, turmeric, ginger, karalla, arum, tomato, and potato[5]	
Triple F Model[3] (simultaneous food, forestry and fish production)			
Rice diversification[5]			Salinity, water logging
Non-traditional crop varieties[4]	Coastal areas	Soybean and sunflower	Salinization

Adaptation method	Areas	Suitable Crops/ Crops Cultivated	Climatic effect
Two crop production cycles[5] Changes in cropping pattern Hanging vegetable garden[6]		Beans, chili, pumpkin	Water logging, salinity infertility

Source:
1 Alauddin and Rahman (2013)
2 Mia (2011)
3 Kibria (2015)
4 Rahman and Islam (2013)
5 Sutradhar *et al.* (2015)
6 Khan (2015)

In summary, arable agriculture adaptation practices already found in the coastal regions include the use of:

- Raised beds: Traditionally grown vegetable crops and fruit trees are planted in raised soil beds, which, after rainfall has removed some of the salt, provide a lower salinity environment at the plant root level and consequently increase the yield (Rahman & Islam, 2013).
- Mound planting: Planting trees on mounds has high potential benefits in combatting the slow onset impacts of climate change, such as sea level rise and saline intrusion (Rahman & Islam, 2013).
- Mulching with organic matter: Mulching helps to increase the retention of soil moisture by reducing evaporation and leaching, effectively diluting any saline water in the soil (Rahman & Islam, 2013).
- Water storage in crop fields: Very effective in dry seasons when salinity increases in the soil and water in the coastal lands (Rahman & Islam, 2013).
- Homestead gardening: A widely accepted practice, mainly managed by women, to increase the overall volume of crop production in the face of declining yields per plant.
- Floating beds: Crops and vegetables are grown on soilless floating platforms made from locally available organic materials such as water hyacinth and other aquatic weeds (Chowdhury & Moore, 2015), essentially as a form of aquaponics.
- Triple F Model (simultaneous food, forestry and fish production): Kibria (2015) reported that mangroves can be introduced around the edges of an elevated homestead to shield against the impact of cyclones, with

vegetables being grown on the protected backyard areas, and fish or shrimp production in associated small ponds (gher) dug out around the house.

- Rice variety diversification: Growing salt tolerant varieties of rice to cope with the increasing salinity, or water-logged conditions in the coastal areas.
- Non-traditional crop varieties: Coastal areas can lack readily available organic manure because of large-scale shrimp farming. Growing non-traditional crops can potentially assist in desalinizing the soil and enriching its quality, and increase the overall productivity.
- Two crop production cycles: Cultivation of sunflower, chickpea and khesari following the cultivation of T. Aman rice can assist in maintaining soil fertility and combatting salinity (Sutradhar *et al.*, 2015).
- Hanging vegetable garden: Vegetables can be grown in pots and on plastic sheeting. Containers are filled with soil mixed with organic compost and placed on roofs, house walls or in extreme cases on trees or frames constructed from local bamboo.

Bangladesh achieved significant progress in agricultural research through improving and innovating newer cop varieties (Anik *et al.*, 2012). The Bangladesh Rice Research Institute (BARI) has developed 57 modern rice varieties. Among the 57 rice varieties 17 are climate resilient. The Bangladesh Institute of Nuclear Agriculture (BINA) has introduced eight high-yielding rice varieties (Table 5.5).

Table 5.5 Rice varieties introduced by BRRI and BINA

Rice variety and released year	Season	Important characteristics	Problem
BRRIdhan 40 (2003)	Aman season	Salt tolerance level: Moderately salt tolerant. Tolerance level up to 8 DS/m during reproductive stage.	Salinity
BRRIdhan 41 (2003)	Aman season	Salt tolerance level: Moderately salt tolerant. Tolerance level up to 8 DS/m during reproductive stage.	Salinity
BRRIdhan 47 (2007)	Boro season	Saline tolerance level: Up to 14 DS/m during seedling stage and 6 DS/m during other growing stages.	Salinity

Rice variety and released year	Season	Important characteristics	Problem
BRRIdhan 51 (2010)	Aman season	Submergence tolerant. Can sustain 12–14 days under water.	Submergence
BRRIdhan 52 (2010)	Aman season	Submergence tolerant.	
BRRIdhan 53 (2010)	Aman season	Salt tolerance level: Saline tolerance level up to 8 DS/m during reproductive stage.	Salinity
BRRIdhan 54 (2010)	Aman season	Salt tolerance level: Saline tolerance level up to 8 DS/m during seedling stage.	Salinity
Binasali (BINA) Binadhan 8 (2012)	Aman season Boro season	Flood and salinity resistance Salt tolerant.	Salinity and flood Salinity and submergence
Binadhan 10	Boro season	Salt tolerant.	Salinity

Source: Alauddin and Rahman (2013); Chowdhury and Hassan (2013); Rahman (2011); Sutradhar *et al.* (2015)

Conclusions

Bangladesh is one of the countries in the world most threatened by the growing impacts of climate change, including the direct effects of rising temperatures and perturbations in rainfall, alongside the impacts of rising sea levels, increased storminess and associated soil and groundwater salinization. Across different economic sectors, arable cultivation of rice, cereals, vegetables and pulses, on which the national economy and the livelihoods of millions of coastal residents are founded, is most seriously threatened. Slowly rising mean sea levels and an apparent increase in the frequency of severe cyclones in particular have rendered the situation acute, and the rate at which farmers are adapting is proving inadequate to fight the battle against climate change. The sector also faces lack of research and funding for experimentation. Most of the published material on arable agriculture is focused on exploring the climate change vulnerabilities of particular crops, whereas the potential modes of adaptation against those vulnerabilities are widely ignored. For example, the effects of climate change on rice production are comparatively well documented, while studies on vulnerabilities of other crops are scarce and what farmers should do or build is not well explored. Floating gardens, ditch-dike systems and the introduction of modified and newer crop varieties are some of the promising adaptation practices for the coastal regions, but they are yet to be widely adopted. The effects of climate change on agriculture are undeniable, and the situation can only worsen if the government and non-government organizations fail to take appropriate actions. Arable agriculture in the Bangladeshi coastal regions urgently needs further research, funding for adaptive measures, appropriate policy and implementation and overall support from both the government and non-government organizations in order to develop climate resilient copping methods, and to survive in the long term.

References

Alam, M., Hossain, M., & Shafee, S. (2003). Frequency of Bay of Bengal cyclonic storms and depressions crossing different coastal zones. *International Journal of Climatology, 23*(9), 1119–1125.

Alauddin, S. M., & Rahman, K. F. (2013). Vulnerability to climate change and adaptation practices in Bangladesh. *Journal of SUB, 4*(2), 25–42.

Ali, A. (2000). *Vulnerability of Bangladesh Coastal Region to Climate Change with Adaptation Option.* Bangladesh Space Research and Remote Sensing Organization (SPARRSO), Dhaka.

Allison, M. A. (1998). Historical changes in the Ganges-Brahmaputra delta front. *Journal of Coastal Research, 14*(4), 1269–1275.

Anik, S. I., Kabir, M. H., & Ray, S. (2012). *Climate Change and Food Security.* Unnayan Onneshan. State of Food Security in Bangladesh. Retrieved from www.unnayan.org/reports/Livelihood/CLIMATE%20CHANGE%20AND%20FOOD%20SECURITY%20_Livelihood%20&%20Food%20Security_uo.pdf

Chowdhury, A. M., Haque, M. A., & Quadir, D. A. (1997). Consequences of global warming and sea level rise in Bangladesh. *Marine Geodesy, 20*(1), 13–31.

Chowdhury, J. U., & Karim, M. F. (1998). *A Rise-Based Zoning of Storm Surge Prone Area of the Ganges Tidal Plain.*

Chowdhury M. A. H. and Hassan M. S. (2013). *Hand book of Agricultural Technology.* Bangladesh Agricultural Research Council, Farmgate, Dhaka. 230p.

Chowdhury, R. B., & Moore, G. A. (2015). Floating agriculture: A potential cleaner production technique for climate change adaptation and sustainable community development in Bangladesh. *Journal of Cleaner Production, 150*, 371–389.

FAO/GIEWS Global Watch. (last updated 21 December 2007). *Livelihood of over 8.9 Million People Adversely Affected by Cyclone Sidr in Bangladesh.* Retrieved from www.fao.org/giews/en/ [Accessed on 15 November 2016].

Global Climate Risk Index (GCRI). (2016). *Who Suffers Most from Extreme Weather Events? Weather-Related Loss Events in 2014 and 1995 to 2014.* Germanwatch. Retrieved from https://germanwatch.org/es/download/13503.pdf [Accessed on 13 March 2018].

Hossain, I. (2013). *Climate Change: A Challenge to Coastal Agriculture in Bangladesh.* Climate Change Adaptation Actions in Bangladesh. Retrieved from www.fao.org/giews/en/ [Accessed on 15 November 2016].

Iftekhar, M. S., & Islam, M. R. (2004). Managing mangroves in Bangladesh: A strategy analysis. *Journal of Coastal Conservation, 10,* 139–146.

Intergovernmental Panel on Climate Change (IPCC). (2001). *Climate Change 2001: The Scientific Basis.* Contribution of Working Group I to the Third Assessment Report of the Intergovernmental Panel on Climate Change [J. T. Houghton, Y. Ding, D. J. Griggs, M. Noguer, P. J. van der Linden, X. Dai, K. Maskell, & C. A. Johnson (Eds.)]. Cambridge, UK and New York, NY, USA: Cambridge University Press, 881pp.

Intergovernmental Panel on Climate Change (IPCC). (2007). *Summary for Policymakers.* Climate Change 2007: Mitigation. Contribution of Working Group III to the Fourth Assessment Report of the Intergovernmental Panel on Climate Change [B. Metz, O. R. Davidson, P. R. Bosch, R. Dave, & L. A. Meyer (Eds.)]. Cambridge, UK and New York, NY, USA: Cambridge University Press.

Islam, M. A., Shitangsu, P. K., & Hassan, M. Z. (2015). Agricultural vulnerability in Bangladesh to climate change induced sea level rise and options for adaptation: A study of a coastal Upazila. *Journal of Agriculture and Environment for International Development, 109*(1), 19–39.

Islam, M. M., & Sado, K. (2000). Flood hazard assessment in Bangladesh using NOAA AVHRR data with geographical information system. *Hydro Process, 14*(3), 605–620.

Islam, T., & Peterson, R. E. (2009). Climatology of landfalling tropical cyclones in Bangladesh 1877–2003. *Natural Hazards, 48*(1), 115–135.

Khalil, G. M. (1993). The catastrophic cyclone of April 1991: Its impact on the economy of Bangladesh. *Natural Hazards, 8*(3), 263–281.

Khan, T.-U.-H. (2015). *Climate change adaptation practices in agriculture: A case study on coastal and drought prone areas of Bangladesh (Dissertation).* Retrieved from http://urn.kb.se/resolve?urn=urn:nbn:se:su:diva-123269

Kibria, G. (2015). *Climate Change Impacts, Actions and Programs (Adaptation & Mitigation) for a Most Vulnerable Country.* Sydneybashi-Bangla.Com Australia, Science & Technology. Article 38. 6p updated. Retrieved from www.sydneybashi-bangla.com/ [Accessed on 10 September 2015].

Mia, M. M. U. (2011). *Adaptation practices for crop production in climate change vulnerable areas in Bangladesh.* Krishi Gobeshona Foundation (KGF). Retrieved from- https://www.scribd.com/document/264014703/12-Project-Code-C-CC-129

Mikhailov, V. N., & Dotsenko, M. A. (2007). Processes of delta formation in the mouth area of the Gangees and Brahmaputra rivers. *Water Resource, 34*(4), 385–400.

Ministry of Environment & Forest (MoEF). (2005). *National Adaptation Program of Action (NAPA).* Government of the People's Republic of Bangladesh.

Nishat, A., & Mukherjee, N. (2013). Climate change impacts, scenario and vulnerability of Bangladesh. In *Climate Change Adaptation Actions in Bangladesh* (pp. 15–41). Tokyo: Springer.

Rahman, M. (2011). *Country Report: Bangladesh.* Retrieved from https://economics.rabobank.com/publications/2011/. . ./country-report-bangladesh/

Rahman, M. M., & Islam, A. (2013). Adaptation technologies in practice and future potentials in Bangladesh. In *Climate Change Adaptation Actions in Bangladesh* (pp. 305–330). Tokyo: Springer.

Saha, D., Hossain, M. S. S., Mondal, M. S., & Rahman, R. (2016). Agricultural adaptation practices in coastal Bangladesh: Response to climate change impacts. *Journal of Modern Science and Technology, 4*(1), 63–74.

Sarwar, M. G. M. (2005). *Impacts of Sea Level Rise on the Coastal Zone of Bangladesh.* Retrieved from http://static.weadapt.org/placemarks/files/225/golam_sarwar.pdf

Sarwar, M. G. M., & Islam, A. (2013). Multi hazard vulnerabilities of the coastal land of Bangladesh. In *Climate change adaptation actions in Bangladesh* (pp. 121–141). Tokyo: Springer.

Shamsuddoha, M., & Chowdhury, R. K. (2007). *Climate Change Impact and Disaster Vulnerabilities in the Coastal Areas of Bangladesh.* Dhaka: COAST Trust.

Sutradhar, L., Bala, S. K., Islam, A. K. M. S., Hasan, M. A., Rahman, M. M., Pavel, M. A. A., & Billah, M. (2015). *A Review of Good Adaptation Practices on Climate Change in Bangladesh.* 5th International Conference on Water & Flood Management (ICWFM).

6 Exploring local drought and adaptation measures in the northwest region of Bangladesh

Md. Shafiqul Islam and Carolyn Roberts

Introduction

Bangladesh is one of the world's regions that is most seriously affected by meteorological disasters such as monsoonal floods, and droughts and tropical cyclones in the pre-and post-monsoon seasons (Rafiuddin *et al.*, 2011). In a country where water is usually plentiful and sometimes present in excess, people nevertheless experience drought and acute water shortages at other times. Drought is probably the least understood of natural hazards, affecting more people globally than any other catastrophe (Wilhite, 2005). This research contributes to the achievement of United Nations Sustainable Development Goal 13 (take urgent action to combat climate change and its impacts) by considering how resilience and adaptive capacity to drought in Bangladeshi villages may be strengthened. It thus relates particularly to Target 13.1 on strengthening resilience and adaptive capacity

Drought is one of the dominant global threats to the environment and people (Dey *et al.*, 2012), and is a relatively common phenomenon in the northwest region of Bangladesh. It is an insidious and capricious natural disaster, lacking even an internationally agreed upon definition. Kapoi and Alabi (2013) have defined 'drought' as a situation of low rainfall relative to normal meteorological conditions, whereas 'water shortage' relates to periods when the demand for water exceeds available supplies, but in practice the terms are often used interchangeably. In the nineteenth century, mass famine followed a drought in 1865, and further dry years and associated impacts on food prices and human mortality followed in various parts of Bangladesh in 1866, 1872 and 1874. Droughts tend to occur in clusters, making analysis of trends over time difficult without long periods of meteorological records; a similar cluster occurred in the 1970s. Droughts periodically affect the northwestern region of the country (Alam, 2015; Patwary & Rahman, 2014), which generally has lower and more variable rainfall than the remainder (Habiba *et al.*, 2011; Ministry of Environment and Forest

[MoEF], 2009; Shahid & Behrawan, 2008). Records show that Bangladesh has experienced some 19 (Habiba *et.al.*, 2011) drought events from 1960 to 1991, a drought once every 1.6 years. Habiba *et al.* (2012) explain that particular human activities (such as over-exploitation of groundwater) may exacerbate water shortages in Bangladesh. A series of studies have identified drought impacts on agriculture (Mazid *et al.*, 2005; Karim *et al.*, 1990), food production (Ericksen *et al.*, 1996; Ahmed & Bernard, 1989) and land degradation (Rasheed, 1998), whilst Tanner *et al.* (2007) has demonstrated that around 2.7 m ha of Bangladesh, almost a third, is vulnerable to annual drought.

According to MoEF (2009), about 83% of crop lands are affected annually by drought during the pre-'*kharif*' (mid-March to mid-July) and dry or '*rabi*' seasons, respectively. Adaptation is derived from the term 'adapt', which means 'making situations better by changing' (Ahmed, 2006). Adaptation to climate change is therefore the process through which people reduce the negative effects of climate on their health and adjust their lifestyles to the situation in which they find themselves (Pender, 2008). For people with limited technology and resources at their disposal, adaptation generally requires being better prepared or adapting to climate change, learning to live with it rather than attempting to fight it. There is an urgent need to map out the options that exist for drought adaptations, and their applicability at the community level in the developing world. This research explores farmer's perceptions of potential drought adaptations, in order to establish adaptation measures at the micro level. As a piece of action research, the specific objectives were to find out the scale and frequency of actual water shortages, to explore the reality of local drought adaptation measures and to enhance local knowledge on drought adaptations.

Methodology

The research was conducted in the semi-arid monsoonal northwest region of Bangladesh, in the Rajshahi Division, close to the Indian border. The region consists of gently undulating land about 20 to 40 m above sea level, receiving about 1,400 to 1,600 mm of rain annually. Rainfall data for a 39-year period was collated from six representative meteorological stations, namely, Manda (Manda station's rainfall data were used for Niamatpur upazila instead of Niamatpur, and there is no station at Niamatpur), Porsha, Tanore, Godagari, Nachole and Shibgonj, and analyzed by calculating a standardized precipitation index (SPI) using the formula developed by Komuscu (1999) for two different periods, namely April–June and July–September. The values of SPI were used in exploring local drought scale, frequency and intensity experienced in the area.

$$SPI = (X - \bar{X})/\sigma$$

Where,
X = Actual Rainfall
$\bar{X}$ = Mean Rainfall
σ = Standard Deviation

In practice, low rainfall is also associated with abnormally high and damaging temperatures, which occasionally reach in excess of 45°C in drought years.

In addition to the local rainfall analysis, six villages were selected from each of six *upazila* (sub-districts) based on the drought severity ranking study of Khan and Islam (2013): the Panihar, Batashpur, Barenda, Kanthalia, Rudrapur and Niskinpur villages. The main occupation of the respondents was agriculture, followed by housewife and business. Monthly average income of the respondents was BDT 8,404.42, and major forms of transport in the villages were rickshaw, *van*, cart, *nosimon* and local bus. The average household size for the village was 4.33 persons. The literacy rate of the villages was 44.53% for both men and women (Bangladesh Bureau of Statistics [BBS], 2011). Community participatory exploration tools were deployed, including household interviews by trained interviewers, 30 in-depth interviews (with officials, farmers, fishermen and elected members), 12 interviews with key informants (with an official from Department of Agricultural Extension and Barind Multipurpose Development Authority) and twelve focus group discussions, to explore local adaptation measures at micro level. A total of 295 households and farms were investigated using population sampling proportionately related to village size, and the collected information was analyzed using Microsoft Excel and the Statistical Package for Social Survey version 20.

Results and discussion

Drought frequency and scale

Annual rainfall totals can be seen in Figure 6.1, from which no unambiguous trends can be identified; although there is a slight overall decline, year-to-year variability is high.

All six of the Rajshahi Division meteorological stations have experienced mild, moderate or more extreme summer droughts within the last 39 years, regardless of which SPI period was used to define drought. Both of the three-month SPIs show that the selected *upazila* experienced mild droughts at least 14 or 15 times between 1976 and 2014 (Figures 6.2 and 6.3), with Tanore station experiencing this situation 17 times; this is approaching once

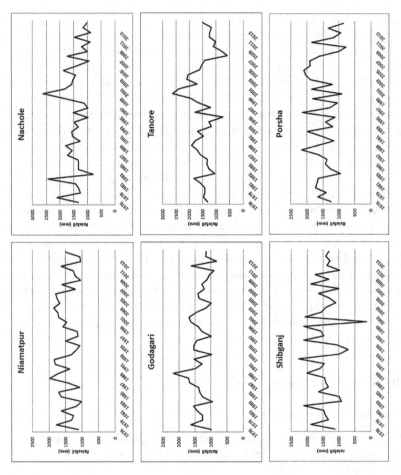

Figure 6.1 Annual rainfalls in the study area

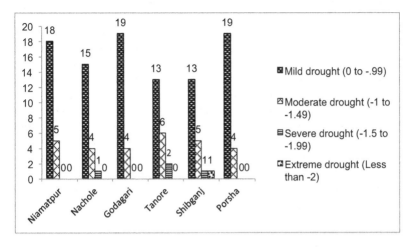

Figure 6.2 Drought frequency and scale using three months (April–June) SPI

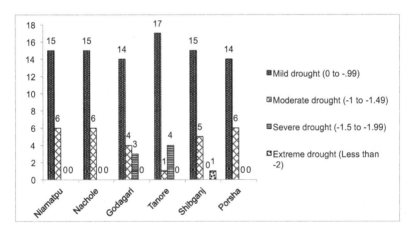

Figure 6.3 Drought frequency and scale using three months (July–September) SPI

every two years. Moreover, Tanore experienced a severe drought four times in the same period, and Godagari did three times; however, the latter also experienced moderate drought an additional four times. On balance, the *upazila* in which Godogari is located has faced the most frequent climatological challenge, with four of the other areas experiencing similar but marginally less severe drought conditions. Farmers working close to Shibganj reported that they experienced more intense drought than others in the region, a position that was partly borne out by the statistical analysis. This showed that Shibganj was the only meteorological station to have recorded an extreme drought (1999), statistically defined, in the years since 1976.

Respondents also perceived and reported that drought frequency in the Rajshahi Division was increasing over the decades, despite the inconclusive statistical evidence for this. This is not unusual, internationally. Modarres and Sarhadi (2009) found a similarly questionable situation when they reviewed long-term annual precipitation trends in Iran; for example, whilst annual rainfall had been decreasing slightly across the country, there were regional differences, and the 24-hour maximum rainfall was increasing concurrently. They suggested that drought had a worldwide return frequency of once every 20–30 years, and on that basis did not suggest significant increases in its frequency in Iran.

Drought intensity

Ninety-eight percent of the Bangladeshi farmers also suggested to interviewers that drought intensity in their area had increased over time, a notably high figure; only 2% of the respondents disagreed with the perspective. All of the respondents in the Batashpur and Kanthalia villages reported their perception that droughts were increasing, with residents in Barenda (98%), Rudrapur (98%), Niskinpur (98%) and Panihar (94%) being progressively less certain. However, the numbers are too small to infer significant differences of perception. Local stations' long-term rainfall data are important in researching local droughts.

Drought and its adaptation measures

Drought support

The questionnaires showed that family or micro-level adaptation measures had been adopted by almost all of the respondents, both in their domestic activities and their farming practices. The direct impact of excessively high temperatures on households' livelihoods and comfort during droughts, for example, had been ameliorated somewhat by technological solutions, particularly the use of mains electricity, fans, air conditioning and refrigerators, but access to these is conditional on having sufficient cash for purchases and running costs. As Patwary and Rahman (2014) reported, people naturally exercise personal choice in mitigating the drought risks, by adjusting (normally reducing) their family food consumption, patterns of eating and daily diets; this is notably challenging in an area that is not wealthy, and individuals do suffer privation and have limited choice. Fifty-five percent of the respondents mentioned that they had received economic and other support from NGOs and relatives during droughts, including seeds, fertilizers, loans and other relief. To minimize economic hardship, some farmers had migrated to other regions temporarily during the drought to secure cash incomes from activities other than farming, leaving their families behind. However, these adaptations are unlikely to be sustainable in the longer term, unless matched by systemic changes in agricultural practices.

Change in the crop calendar

Drought-related changes in agricultural practices in the Rajshahi Division have been identified. Respondents mentioned that their crop calendar for planting and harvesting times had changed as a result of their perceptions of the increased risk of drought. Depending on the nature of the cultivation, farmers had started their cultivation either earlier or later in the cropping season to accommodate the possibility of drought risks.

The extent of adjustment in cropping season (time) varied between the respondents, with almost everyone reporting that they had made some changes in recent years, usually by beginning to cultivate earlier in the cropping season, to take advantage of greater potential availability of water and lower temperatures. Only 3% of the reported adjustments were in the limited range of between five and ten days, which might be expected to lie within the normal range for farmers' convenience from year to year. However, 50% of the farmers reported that they had brought their cultivation time forward by between 11 and 15 days, 12% by between 16 and 20 days and 19% by between 21 days and a month. A further 2% of the respondents reported that they attempted to reduce drought damage by delaying their cultivation time by between 11 and 15 days, 13% by deferring their cultivation time by between 16 and 20 days, 6% by between 21 and 30 days and a very small number by over a month. The different adjustment tactics of earlier or later planting relate in part to the variety of crops being cultivated to reduce drought impacts. As mentioned by the respondents, if they do so (earlier sowing/planting) they can take advantages of soil moisture for germination and seedling survivability.

Farmers apply various agricultural strategies to reduce the impacts of water shortages on their livelihoods, the extent of adaptation being dependent on several factors including the perceived frequency, intensity and spatial scale of dry periods. In theory, adaptation can occur at the macro- (national), meso- (local) and micro- (village, community and household) levels. However, the micro-level individual adjustments of '*what the farmers do in response to drought*' are of prime importance, as Keshavarz *et al.* (2010) have noted. Uddin *et al.*'s (2014) research suggests that typically six principal factors (the respondent's age, family size, farm size, education, family income and cooperative involvement) are statistically significant in relation to the adoption of particular adaptive strategies. Depending on the circumstances, adjustments potentially include optimizing the use of land, selecting the most suitable cultivars, ploughing land deeply before drought to introduce water-holding voids, using composted manure to improve the physical properties of the soil and digging ponds to create water storage reservoirs. Few applications have a limited impact on drought mitigation and increase farmers' responsibility during drought (Burton *et al.*, 1998). The areas that experience greater drought frequency, at Godagari and at Shibgonj, which may have had more intense droughts, have different adaptation strategies.

Suitable cultivar

According to the findings of this study, many farmers have adjusted their crops to accommodate the risk of drought, and anticipated doing more in the future. A clear majority (85%) believed that wheat was well adapted to grow in drought-prone areas, followed in popularity by mustard (63%), corn (53%), lentils (37%), potato (23%), linseed (22%), the pulse *masakalai* (14%), paddy rice (7%) and sugarcane (5%). Farmers fearing drought attempt to choose a crop that is more adaptive, multifunctional and high yielding (Ju *et al.*, 2008), although their choices are not always proved to be appropriate. Some crops in the northern region of Bangladesh are relatively drought-tolerant, such as millet *('coun')* mentioned by the respondents (in-depth interview), some edible oilseed crops (*teel, tishi, kalijira*) and a number of local rice varieties mentioned by respondents (KIIs). They learnt by doing it themselves and getting information from Department of Agricultural Extension (DAE).

Compost and organic fertilizer

Local farmers have also paid some attention to the possibilities afforded by moving to a more organic form of cultivation, specifically in relation to the use of composts, as a response to drought. They alluded to soil in the study areas being 'exhausted' (that is, having low fertility due to low nutrient and organic matter levels) and suggested that the addition of compost was beneficial, in part as protection against extended dry periods. Eighty-one percent of the respondents mentioned that organic fertilizer increased soil fertility, leading to increased crop yields (74%), enhanced soil moisture retention (24%) and decreased environmental pollution (5%). The results are summarized in Table 6.1. Whilst farmers in the different *upazila* ranked the benefits similarly overall, those in Rudrapur and Batashpur

Table 6.1 Benefits of organic fertilizers

Benefits of organic agriculture	Rajshahi		Chapai Nawabganj		Naogaon		Total N = 295
	Panihar n = 33	Batashpur n = 55	Barenda n = 59	Kanthalia n = 32	Rudrapur n = 56	Niskinpur n = 60	
Fertility increase	81.8	74.1	96.6	100	48.2	96.6	81.36
Production increase	66.7	63	52.5	100	73.2	100	74.24
Soil moisture increase	69.7	16.7	10.2	31.2	33.9	6.8	24.07
Decrease environment pollution	12.1		1.7		19.6		5.42

Source: Field survey 2015 (multiple responses)
Notes: *n* = number, *N* = Total number of respondents

were somewhat less convinced of the benefits of compost incorporation. Those in Kanthalia, Niskinpur and Barenda were very keen to highlight the associated soil fertility increases, whilst in Rudrapur the most commonly mentioned benefit was crop production increases. Rudrapur and Panihar farmers also touched on the possibility of decreased environmental pollution, in comparison with artificial fertilizers, more commonly than those living elsewhere; for farmers in most of the *upazila* this was not a concern. The farmers believe that the use of chemical fertilizers makes soil dry and hard; the farmers' emphasis on soil moisture in Panihar related to drought, using compost or organic fertilizers.

Drought loss recovery process

Farmers generally attempted to recover their losses after droughts, using a variety of methods dependent upon their perception of the available options and the severity of the situation, although some 4% of the farmers, mainly in Batashpur village, claimed that they could not recover from the drought and that their livelihoods had been permanently damaged. The results of the interviews are summarized in Table 6.2. Immediate economic adjustments were the most significant; farmers in every *upazila* mentioned taking loans from NGOs, with 54% overall being reliant on this support. Those in Kanthalia were notably dependent on such loans, with every respondent having borrowed from an NGO, whereas in Batashpur and Niskinpur fewer than half had done so. Farmers in Radrapur and Panihar were also heavily dependent on borrowing from other lenders, a practice not common

Table 6.2 Available options to recover from drought loss

Drought recovery measures	Rajshahi		Chapai Nawabganj		Naogaon		Total N = 295
	Panihar n = 33	Batashpur n = 55	Barenda n = 59	Kanthalia n = 32	Rudrapur n = 56	Niskinpur n = 60	
Cattle rearing		40.7	69	34.4	41.1	76.3	47.80
Fish cultivation	9.4	3.7				16.9	5.08
Small trading		3.7	1.7		1.8		1.36
NGO loan	50	35.2	55.2	100	60.7	44.1	53.90
By working	68.8	16.7	1.7		3.6		11.53
Business		3.7			1.8		1.02
Can't recover		16.7	1.7			1.7	3.73
Tuition		1.9					0.34
Selling property		1.9			3.6		1.02
Loan from others	65.6	5.6			67.9		21.02

Source: Field survey 2015 (multiple responses)
Notes: n = number, N = Total number of respondents

elsewhere. A majority of Panihar farmers (69%), and some in Batashpur (17%) also mentioned changing their work, a practice much less common elsewhere. Small numbers had sold property (1% across all the villages), started small trading enterprises (1%) or started other businesses (1%) to recover from drought.

In terms of changing agricultural practices, beginning cattle rearing (for milk and income) was the second most popular option to recover the loss following drought, except in Panihar where it was unknown (a lack of grazing land and fodder was assumed). Cattle rearing is particularly popular in Niskinpur and Barenda, where it was mentioned by 76% and 69% of the farmers, respectively. In Niskinpur, Panihar and Batashpur, a minority of farmers had also begun to cultivate fish as a response to drought, although overall numbers doing so were limited (17%, 9% and 4% of the respondents, respectively). These practices made them capable of leading their livelihoods and combating drought successfully over the generations.

Conclusion and recommendation

This exploration of micro-level adaptation in an area of northwest Bangladesh, where droughts vary in intensity and associated water shortages are a common occurrence, has demonstrated some of the variability in local responses. Respondents have known drought, and generally adapted their lives and livelihoods to it using local knowledge, throughout their lives. They generally believe droughts to be increasing in frequency or severity, and local adaptation has included changes in cropping calendars, organic farming and drought loss recovery processes. Nevertheless, there is still a clear knowledge gap related to a wider range of potential drought adaptations, or of services which could be made available centrally or locally to mitigate the situation. Focus group discussions suggested that absent or inadequate agricultural extension and advisory services, limited drought prediction and forecasting services, poor local knowledge of improved crop varieties, lack of subsidies for appropriate seeds and fertilizers, limited knowledge of adaptation measures and low institutional capacity are hindering drought adaptation.

The following recommendations are made based on the research:

- There are some misconceptions and uncertainties regarding drought adaptation issues. These should be made clearer to farmers through knowledge sharing and capacity building. Skill development training on drought adaptation measures could be provided for farmers through 'field schools' and yard meetings.
- Farmers could collaborate further by fighting drought impacts through their own initiatives, for example, shared water storage systems.
- Consideration could be given to drought insurance in the study area, in order to sustain victims' livelihoods in the event of an extreme event.
- Incentives for organic agriculture, where this can be shown to improve soil moisture retention, should be established in the study areas for better management of drought.
- Drought is a complex matter, involving different combinations and climatological circumstances as well as multiple stakeholders, and having serious consequences. More research is urgently required on the compatibility of a mixture of drought adaptation measures, to avoid unexpected consequences from single adaptations that may prove unsustainable.

References

Ahmed, A. U. (2006). *Bangladesh Climate Change Impacts and Vulnerability: A Synthesis*. Dhaka, Bangladesh: Climate Change Cell, Department of Environment.

Ahmed, R., & Bernard, A. (1989). *Rice Price Fluctuation and an Approach to Price Stabilization in Bangladesh* (Vol. 72). Washington, D.C.: Intl Food Policy Res Inst.

Alam, K. (2015). Farmers' adaptation to water scarcity in drought-prone environments: A case study of Rajshahi district, Bangladesh. *Agricultural Water Management*, *148*, 196–206.

Bangladesh Bureau of Statistics (BBS). (2011). *Population & Housing Census 2011: Preliminary Results*. July 2011, Bangladesh Bureau of Statistics, Statistics Division, Ministry of Planning, Government of the People's Republic of Bangladesh.

Burton, I., Smith, J. B., & Lenhart, S. (1998). Adaptation to climate change: Theory and assessment. In *Handbook on Methods for Climate Change Impact Assessment and Adaptation Strategies* (pp. 5-1–5-20). Nairobi, Kenya: United Nations Environment Programme.

Dey, N. C., Alam, M. S., Sajjan, A. K., Bhuiyan, M. A., Ghose, L., Ibaraki, Y., & Karim, F. (2012). Assessing environmental and health impact of drought in the Northwest Bangladesh. *Journal of Environmental Science and Natural Resources*, *4*(2), 89–97.

Ericksen, N. J., Ahmad, Q. K., & Chowdhury, A. R. (1996). Socio-economic implications of climate change for Bangladesh. In *The Implications of Climate and Sea-Level Change for Bangladesh* (pp. 205–287). Dordrecht: Springer.

Habiba, U., Shaw, R., & Takeuchi, Y. (2011). Drought risk reduction through a socio-economic, institutional and physical approach in the northwestern region of Bangladesh. *Environmental Hazards*, *10*(2), 121–138.

Habiba, U., Shaw, R., & Takeuchi, Y. (2012). Farmer's perception and adaptation practices to cope with drought: Perspectives from Northwestern Bangladesh. *International Journal of Disaster Risk Reduction*, *1*, 72–84.

Ju, H., Conway, D., Li, Y., Harvey, A., Lin, E., & Calsamiglia-Mendlewicz, S. (2008). *Adaptation Framework and Strategy Part 2: Application of the Adaptation Framework: A Case Study of Ningxia, Northwest China*.

Kapoi, K. J., & Alabi, O. (2013, November). Agricultural drought severity assessment using Land surface temperature and NDVI in Nakuru region, Kenya. In *Proceedings of Global Geospatial Conference, Addis Ababa, Ethiopia* (pp. 4–8). Ethiopia.

Karim, Z., Ibrahim, A., Iqbal, A., & Ahmed, M. (1990). Drought in Bangladesh agriculture and irrigation schedules for major crops. *Bangladesh Agricultural Research Center (BARC) Publication*, *34*.

Keshavarz, M., Karami, E., & Kamgare-Haghighi, A. (2010). A typology of farmers' drought management. *American-Eurasian Journal of Agriculture & Environmental Sciences*, *7*(4), 415–426.

Khan, M. F. A., & Islam, M. S. (2013). *Vulnerability to Climate Induced Drought: Scenario and Impacts*. CDMP.

Komuscu, U. A. (1999). Using the SPI to analyze spatial and temporal patterns of drought in Turkey. *Drought Network News (1994–2001)*, *49*.

Mazid, M. A., Mortimer, M. A., Riches, C. R., Orr, A., Karmaker, B., Ali, A., & Wade, L. J. (2005). Rice establishment in drought-prone areas of Bangladesh. In *Rice Is Life: Scientific Perspectives for the 21st Century*. Los Banos, Philippines: Proceedings of the World Rice Research Conference.

Ministry of Environment and Forests (MoEF). (2009). *Strategy, B. C. C., and Plan, A*. Ministry of Environment and Forests. Government of the People's Republic of Bangladesh, Dhaka, Bangladesh.

Modarres, R., & Sarhadi, A. (2009). Rainfall trends analysis of Iran in the last half of the twentieth century. *Journal of Geophysical Research: Atmospheres, 114*(D3).

Patwary, M. A., & Rahman, M. A. (2014). Food security through food habit change as an adaptation process to climate change. *British Journal of Applied Science and Technology, 4*(32), 4494.

Pender, J. S. (2008). *What Is Climate Change?: And How It Will Effect Bangladesh*. Dhaka: Church of Bangladesh Social Development Programme.

Rafiuddin, M., Dash, B. K., Khanam, F., & Islam, M. N. (2011, April). *Diagnosis of Drought in Bangladesh Using Standardized Precipitation Index*. 2011 International Conference on Environment Science and Engineering.

Rasheed, K. B. S. (1998, April). *Status of Land Resource Use and Desertification, Drought and Land Degradation in Bangladesh: Obstacles and Effective Policy Options and Measures for Sustainable Use of Land Resources*. Proceedings of the National Awareness Seminar on Combating Land Degradation/Desertification in Bangladesh.

Shahid, S., & Behrawan, H. (2008). Drought risk assessment in the western part of Bangladesh. *Natural Hazards, 46*(3), 391–413.

Tanner, T. M., Hassan, A., Islam, K. N., Conway, D., Mechler, R., Ahmed, A. U., & Alam, M. (2007). ORCHID: Piloting climate risk screening in DFID Bangladesh. In *Institute of Development Studies Research Report*. Brighton, UK: IDS.

Uddin, M. N., Bokelmann, W., & Entsminger, J. S. (2014). Factors affecting farmers' adaptation strategies to environmental degradation and climate change effects: A farm level study in Bangladesh. *Climate, 2*(4), 223–241.

Wilhite, D. A. (2005). The role of disaster preparedness in national planning with specific reference to droughts. In *Natural Disasters and Extreme Events in Agriculture* (pp. 23–37). Berlin and Heidelberg: Springer.

7 Household level coping strategies for flood disaster

A study on the Padma River Islands of Bangladesh

Rumana Sultana, Md. Shafiul Alam and Samiya Ahmed Selim

Introduction

Flooding, one of the most catastrophic natural disasters, is reported to have accounted for 6.8 million deaths worldwide in the twentieth century (Jonkman & Kelman, 2005). The impact of natural hazards has been increasing significantly over the last decades, and in Bangladesh it is assumed that this is mostly the consequence of climatic change (Fenton *et al.*, 2017; Intergovernmental Panel on Climate Change [IPCC], 2013). The occurrence of floods has increased over the past decades, with enormous public health implications and massive alterations to the lives of those affected (Osuret *et al.*, 2016). Bangladesh experiences severe exposure to river flooding due to its geomorphological, demographic and socio-economic characteristics (Agrawala *et al.*, 2003). Lying on the massive delta of the Ganges, Brahmaputra and Meghna Rivers, and underlain mainly by soft alluvial materials, monsoonal flooding is to be expected annually in much of the country. Moderate-frequency floods are widely viewed as a blessing by Bangladeshis because they bring economic and environmental benefits for agriculture and wildlife (Handmer *et al.*, 1999; Smith, 1996; Blaikie *et al.*, 1994), whereas the less frequent, high-magnitude events are often disastrous (Paul, 1997), causing widespread loss of life, illness and economic upheaval. Approximately 60% of the country's land area is less than six meters above mean sea level (Government of Bangladesh [GOB], 1992; United States Agency for International Development [USAID], 1988), and flood water typically inundates around 21% of the country (3.03 million ha) between June and September every year (Mirza *et al.*, 2001). In extreme cases it may cover 70% of the country (Mirza, 2002), with varied effects. Households in low-lying riverine areas are obviously more exposed to frequent flooding than those in the higher areas of the country lying mainly in the east and far north (Alam *et al.*, 2017; Alam *et al.*, 2016), but these latter areas, too, can experience flash flooding from intense rainfall.

The river floods of 1951, 1954, 1955 and 1974 caused enormous damages to properties and considerable loss of life, but the floods of 1987, 1988, 1998, 2004 and 2007 were even more catastrophic (Flood Forecasting & Warning Center [FFWC], 2016; GOB, 2006). The 1998 floods in particular inundated some 75% of the country for 15–20 days when flows in the three major rivers of the area peaked synchronously. Half of the capital, Dhaka, was affected and up to 30 million people rendered homeless. As a consequence, government and non-governmental organizations in Bangladesh have attempted to utilize structural or engineered approaches (embankments, levees and polders, for instance) alongside non-structural measures (such as awareness raising and flood warning) for flood prevention and mitigation (Paul, 1997). A major concern is that none of the structural methods are particularly effective against large floods, and they may not be economically viable in the developing world, or environmentally friendly either (Paul & Routray, 2009). Adaptation strategies seem more likely to offer a more sustainable solution, by helping people to cope better with climatic variations and associated weather-related disasters (Alam *et al.*, 2016; Niles *et al.*, 2015; Gandure *et al.*, 2013; Adger *et al.*, 2003). There has been recent consideration of the flood mitigation strategies of local Indigenous peoples (Osuret *et al.*, 2016; Sultana & Rayhan, 2012; Paul, 2010; Blaikie *et al.*, 1994), as they appear able to be implemented quickly and more sustainably (Benson *et al.*, 2001; Few, 2003). Both 'preventative' measures taken before a trigger event and 'mitigative' measures during and after a flood (Paul & Routray, 2009) have been of interest. In addition, other coping strategies provide the fallback mechanisms when habitual means of meeting needs are disrupted, as Frankenberger (1992) has pointed out. Coping responses and adjustment strategies to disasters (Mallick *et al.*, 2009; Paul & Routray, 2009) include adjustments both to the physical infrastructure, that is the property, buildings, land and infrastructure, and to social conditions (Paul, 2012; Islam *et al.*, 2011).

If triggered by a flood, or the prospect of a flood, poor households will attempt to expend the minimum amount of resources required to survive and recover (Sultana & Rayhan, 2012). The major objective of this study is thus to explore not only the economic and technological coping strategies used to combat flood disaster and maintain a sustainable life, at the household level, but also the social adaptations. Whilst numerous studies have focused on the vulnerability of populations to climatic changes and natural hazards, (Islam *et al.*, 2017; Islam *et al.*, 2016; Emrich & Cutter, 2011; Adger, 2006), and some have focused on the community level (Sultana & Rayhan, 2012; Paul & Routray, 2009), research at the scale of individual households is very limited. Yet household-level tactics are a cross-cutting research issue in the context of sustainable development, and are a particularly valuable tool for addressing the United Nations Sustainable Development Goal 13, relating to the need for urgent action to combat the implications of climate change, specifically targeting 13.1, which covers the need to strengthen resilience and adaptive capacity to climate-related hazards and natural disasters in all countries.

Study area and methodology

The Padma River is the major distributary of the Ganges, meandering eastward from the Indian border through the western areas of Bangladesh. The river migrates periodically across a wide floodplain, eroding and removing some silty areas, and depositing others. It has an annual cycle of flooding, driven mainly by monsoonal rain in the upper parts of the catchment, and water typically rises over a period of a few days, progressively inundating the floodplain areas. From 1960 to 2012, havoc floods (50,001–60,000 cumecs) occurred 22 times in the Padma River basin area (Sultana *et al.*, 2013). The Indian Farakka barrage has reduced average water levels somewhat in low flow conditions, making the river less navigable, but it remains a powerful agent of change in communities.

Based on their vulnerability to floods, five Padma River island villages from Narayanpur Mauza in the Nawabganj district of the country, between 24°30' to 24°33' North and 88°05' to 88°09' East, were selected for this study: Narayanpur, Satrashia, Madrasa Para, Debpur and Narayanpur Ghon (Figure 7.1). The small villages are typical of many others in this region, their residents being dependent for their livelihoods principally on irrigated agriculture, mango cultivation and some fishing. Household incomes and levels of literacy (particularly for women) are relatively low, even within Bangladesh, but have been rising recently according to World Bank statistics. Villagers generally have no access to television and internet.

The primary research data was collected in 2013 through household questionnaire surveys, and observation. Following a simple random sampling process, 178 households were selected from the villages, subsamples being generated in proportion to the size of each of the five villages (Yamane, 1967). A number of potential social, economic and technological coping strategies were identified in advance of the survey, based on impact assessment and literature on mitigation for natural hazards in similar study areas (Osuret *et al.*, 2016; Sultana & Rayhan, 2012; Paul & Routray, 2009; Adger, 2006; Bollin & Hidajat, 2003). Residents were asked to score their deployment of each strategy when faced with a trigger event such as a flood (Davis, 1996), based on a five-point Likert scale (prepared by assigning a value of 1 (very rare) through 5 (very often); "0" was given when the strategy did not apply). The scaled values were averaged to get a single mean value for each coping strategy, and for each village.

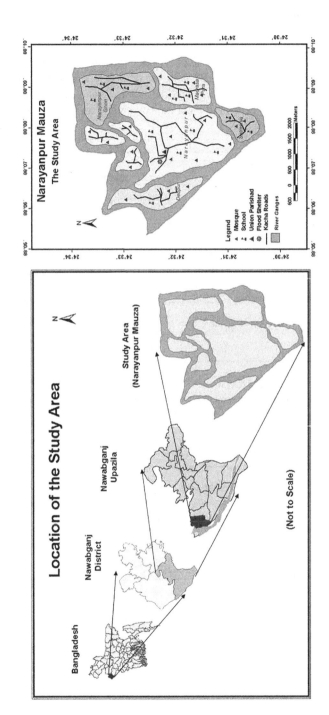

Figure 7.1 Location of the study area
partially adopted from Sultana and Alam, 2016

Results and discussion

The research identified the patterns of coping strategies adopted by the different households to reduce the negative impact of disasters, and the results are presented in Figures 7.2, 7.3 and 7.4, and Tables 7.1, 7.2 and 7.3, separated into economic, social and technological adjustments. Previous literature

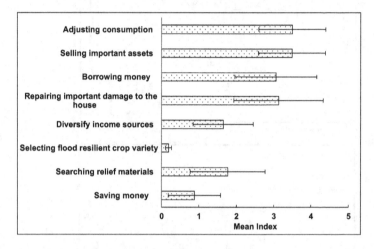

Figure 7.2 Mean and Standard deviation (*SD*) of economic coping strategies (all villages). Criteria of assessment were 1 = Very rare, 2 = Rare, 3 = Moderate, 4 = Often and 5 = Very often. "0" was given when strategy did not apply.

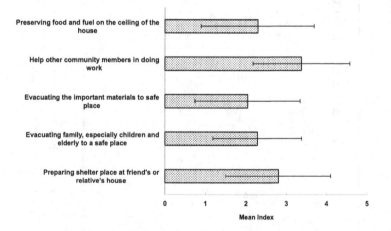

Figure 7.3 Mean and *SD* of social coping strategies (all villages). Criteria of assessment were 1 = Very rare, 2 = Rare, 3 = Moderate, 4 = Often and 5 = Very often. "0" was given when strategy did not apply.

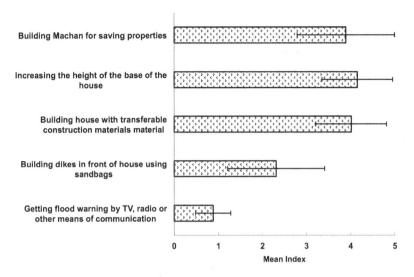

Figure 7.4 Mean and *SD* of technological or structural coping strategies (all villages). Criteria of assessment were 1 = Very rare, 2 = Rare, 3 = Moderate, 4 = Often and 5 = Very often. "0" was given when strategy did not apply.

(Osuret *et al.*, 2016; Sultana & Rayhan, 2012) suggests that economic coping mechanisms play the most significant role in reducing the negative impact of flood disaster, but in the case of the Padma River island villages, technological strategies are more strongly rated overall (Table 7.3), perhaps as a result of the specific physical circumstances of the village settings.

Economic coping strategies

Households in the five Narayanpur Mauza villages have developed their own individual economic coping strategies to prepare for, and guard against, flooding (usually last for one month), but common themes emerged from the research. Adjusting (basically reducing) consumption of food and other goods, and selling important household assets (e.g., furniture, livestock, gold ornaments), were universally the most characteristic responses to a flood disaster, with all the households reporting that they reduced the already limited amount of food consumed, and the clothes they bought. Narayanpur Ghon and Debpur village residents scored this response particularly high. A previous study by Sultana and Rayhan (2012) also reported that 154 flooded households in this region of Bangladesh had reduced the number of meals eaten and their daily amount consumed, or that they sometimes bought cheaper food items to cope with flood damage.

Table 7.1 Economic coping strategies (breakdown of villages). Criteria of assessment were 1 = Very rare, 2 = Rare, 3 = Moderate, 4 = Often and 5 = Very often. "0" was given when strategy did not apply

Economic coping strategies	Villages									
	Narayanpur		Satrashia		Madrasa Para		Debpur		Narayanpur Ghom	
	Mean Index	SD	Mean Index	SD	Mean Index	SD	Mean Index	SD	Mean Index	SD
Saving money	0.70	0.8	0.74	1.1	1.33	1	1.00	0.9	1.20	1
Searching relief materials	1.92	0.9	1.87	1	1.60	0.9	1.42	0.9	1.27	1.1
Selecting flood resilient crop variety	0.16	0.4	0.22	0.4	0.13	1	0.25	0.4	0.40	0.7
Diversify income sources	1.60	0.4	1.74	0.8	1.63	0.7	1.75	0.9	1.73	0.8
Repairing important damage to the house	3.07	0.9	3.30	1.2	3.40	1.2	2.67	1.4	3.13	1.4
Borrowing money	3.01	0.9	2.35	1.1	2.93	1.4	4.00	0.8	3.93	1.2
Selling important assets	3.35	0.7	3.65	0.9	3.50	1	3.75	1.2	4.00	0.8
Adjusting consumption	3.35	0.7	3.65	0.9	3.60	1.1	3.7	1.1	3.93	1.2
Grand mean for villages	2.14		2.03		2.27		2.32		2.45	
Grand mean of economic coping strategies							2.24			

Table 7.2 Social coping strategies (breakdown of villages). Criteria of assessment were 1 = Very rare, 2 = Rare, 3 = Moderate, 4 = Often and 5 = Very often. "0" was given when strategy did not apply

Social coping strategies	Villages									
	Narayanpur		Satrashia		Madrasa Para		Debpur		Narayanpur Ghon	
	Mean Index	SD	Mean Index	SD	Mean Index	SD	Mean Index	SD	Mean Index	SD
Preparing shelter place at a friend's or relative's house	2.78	1.2	2.74	1.4	2.63	1.3	3.08	1.4	3.20	1.6
Evacuating family, especially children and the elderly, to a safe place	2.35	1	2.13	1.1	2.53	1.4	1.83	1.4	1.87	1.1
Evacuating is the important thing to get to safe place	1.96	1	1.87	1.2	2.50	1.3	1.82	1.3	2.07	1.6
Help other community members in doing work	3.60	1.1	2.87	1.4	3.37	1.5	2.83	1.5	3.07	1.5
Preserving food and fuel on the ceiling of the house	2.20	1.3	2.09	1.5	2.77	1.5	2.42	1.6	2.07	1.1
Grand mean for villages	2.58		2.34		2.76		2.40		2.46	
Grand mean of social coping strategies			2.51							

Table 7.3 Technological or structural strategies (breakdown of villages). Criteria of assessment were 1 = Very rare, 2 = Rare, 3 = Moderate, 4 = Often and 5 = Very often. "0" was given when strategy did not apply

Technological or structural coping strategies	Villages											
	Narayanpur		Satrashia		Madrasa Para		Debpur		Narayanpur Ghon		
	Mean Index	SD	Mean Index	SD	Mean Index	SD	Mean Index	SD	Mean Index	SD
Getting flood warnings by TV, radio or other means of communication	0.66	0.2	0.57	0.3	1.50	0.7	1.50	0.8	1.01	0.6
Building dikes in front of the house using sandbags	2.39	1	2.26	1.4	1.90	1	2.25	1.1	2.80	1.4
Building the house with transferable construction materials	3.55	1	4.13	0.9	3.72	1.2	3.75	1.2	3.33	1.3
Increasing the height of the base of the house	4.75	0.8	4.39	1.1	4.01	1	3.92	1.3	4.50	0.9
Building *Machan* for saving properties	4.02	0.9	4.22	1	3.60	1.1	3.31	1.3	4.01	1.1
Grand mean for villages	3.07		3.11		2.95		2.94		3.13	
Grand mean for technological coping strategies					3.04					

95% of the households borrowed money to survive, a figure that is consistent with the findings of Ninno *et al.* (2001) from research undertaken two decades ago, and repairing significant damage to the household buildings was another strategy that local people deployed very often. Conversely, more than 95% of the households reported that they had no idea about cultivating flood resilient crop varieties, and that this strategy was very rarely used. Saving money in times of relative plenty is another potential coping strategy, but in the present study area it was rarely utilized, households (21%) rarely using any savings to cope with flood because they generally had no savings. Very little effort was expended by any respondents to seek support (materials or money) from relief agencies.

Somewhat different economic responses were noted in the five villages. Whilst Narayanpur Ghon and Debpur residents tended to favour passive strategies such as consuming less, selling assets and borrowing money, Madrasa Para and Satrashia residents invested time and resources in house repairs (Table 7.1). On the other hand, Narayanpur Ghon, Debpur and Satrashia residents paid some attention to diversifying their sources of income, although Satrashia residents were not commonly using economic tactics to accommodate the flood risk. They were not generally saving money in preparation for a flood, but borrowing afterwards. Satrashia showed the lowest mean index in the case of borrowing money. Saving money was ranked highest in the households of Madrasa Para.

Social coping strategies

Across the five villages, utilization of social coping strategies was rated somewhat more highly than economic strategies, receiving higher overall scores. Some of the previous literature has suggested that in flood affected localities, coping starts with direct efforts to save peoples' lives, such as work to raise the ground level of a homestead before a flood (Thompson & Tod, 1998; Rasid & Paul, 1987), and this also proved to be the case here. However, among the social coping strategies recorded in the Padma River islands, helping other community members in doing work was the most highly ranked response, particularly in the Narayanpur and Madrasa Para villages where people work together on projects; Debpur residents were slightly less likely to highly rate assisting their neighbours, but the relative emphasis is not significantly different to the other villages. Preserving food and fuel on the ceiling or roof of the house represented the second highest score, in this case, again, a tactic particularly common in Madrasa Para; Narayanpur residents are much less likely to do this. In Narayanpur mauza generally, 45% of all households preserve food and fuel on the ceiling of the house very often. Conversely, evacuating important materials to safe places showed the lowest scored mean value (2.04 average), with evacuating vulnerable residents scoring only marginally higher (2.28); village residents view family members as being at relatively low risk. In Madrasa Para, evacuation of important materials (i.e., livestock, money and furniture) to safe places, and evacuating family members, is scored highest, whereas in Debpur both of these strategies are ranked low (Table 7.2). Among the villages, the scores for preparing shelter places at friends' and relatives' houses were moderate, highest in Narayanpur Ghon village and lowest in Madrasa Para. In the Narayanpur Mauza villages' households those who have access to a mosque (a shelter during flood), schools and good social networks can utilize social strategies often. However, previously it was reported that access to institutions and social capital can enhance poor households' adaptation choices (Alam *et al.*, 2017, 2017; Jordan, 2015).

Technological or structural coping strategies

The use of technological or structural coping mechanisms was scored comparatively more highly than other types of coping strategies across the Padma River island villages. Increasing the height of the base of the house by piling up earth attracted the highest-scored mean value (Figures 7.4). Narayanpur residents are most likely to expend considerable effort in building these structures, and those in Debpur village are the least. Similarly, building houses with transferable and reusable construction materials (i.e., straw, mud, tin, wood, polyethylene) was given the second highest mean score, particularly by Satrashia residents (Table 7.3). These materials can be rescued and recycled if property damage is severe, but they are left on the site as the water level drops. Building *'machan'*, temporary wooden or bamboo platforms around trees or other structures, to keep people above the water level, attracted the third highest average score (Figure 7.4), being relatively straightforward to accomplish. These structures were most popular in Satrashia, and least popular in Debpur, as the villagers of Satrashia will need more than three hours to evacuate important materials to flood shelters.

Flood warnings from television, radio or other means of communication are not highly scored overall; responses are marginally more positive for households in the Madrasa Para village and Debpur villages. This may suggest inadequate penetration of the warnings to all villages, or lack of residents' access to broadcast material. Less than 20% of the respondents usually get a flood warning. Additionally, the construction of temporary dikes around homes using earth or sandbags is not common in this area, which generated the second lowest value (Figure 7.4), indicating that people in Narayanpur mauza do not usually use this Indigenous structural strategy to overcome the negative impacts of floods. The scored mean value for building dikes around the house is nevertheless higher than average in Narayanpur Ghon village and lower in Madrasa Para (Table 7.3).

Period of use of coping mechanisms

Previous literature has reported that coping strategies are mostly taken during the disaster and post-disaster period (Sultana & Rayhan, 2012; Paul & Routary, 2009). Here however, some coping strategies such as increasing the height of the base of the house and building *machan* (wooden platforms) for saving property and people are preventive and are utilized in the pre-disaster period. Table 7.4 shows the utilization of economic, social and technological coping strategies in three periods of the disaster management

Table 7.4 Period of use of coping mechanism

Coping Mechanism	Period of Use		
	Pre-Disaster	During Disaster	Post Disaster
Economic Coping Strategies			
Saving money	■		
Searching for relief materials			■
Selecting flood resilient crop variety	■		
Diversifying income sources	■	■	■
Repairing important damage to the house			■
Borrowing money			■
Selling important assets			■
Adjusting consumption			■
Social Coping Strategies			
Preparing shelter at friend's or relative's house	■		
Evacuating family, especially children and the elderly, to a safe place		■	
Evacuating the important things to a safe place	■	■	
Helping other community members in doing work		■	■
Preserving food and fuel on the ceiling of the house	■	■	

(*Continued*)

Table 7.4 (Continued)

Coping Mechanism	Period of Use		
	Pre-Disaster	During Disaster	Post Disaster
Technological or Structural Coping Strategies			
Getting flood warnings by TV, radio or other means of communication	▉		
Building dikes in front of the house using sandbags	▉		
Building the house with transferable construction materials	▉		
Increasing the height of the base of the house	▉		
Building *Machan* for saving properties	▉		▉

Source: Sultana *et al.* 2013

cycle. Almost all of the structural or technological coping strategies come into play in the pre-disaster period since they require time for construction or to establish links for technologically brokered communications, whereas most of the economic coping strategies (such as searching for relief materials and diversifying income sources) are necessarily used only in post-disaster periods. Social coping strategies are used in all three periods of the disaster management cycle since utilization of these were found easier and least costly by the surveyed households.

Conclusion

Our results revealed that flood-prone households in the Padma River islands exhibit multiple responses for coping with flood disaster, with typical answers varying somewhat from village to village. Household-level economic, social and technological strategies are all influential in reducing the negative impact of flood disasters. The greatest numbers of households have to reduce their consumption of food and clothes, sell important assets (i.e., livestock, gold ornaments) and borrow money after flood events, in order to survive the damage to their crops, houses and possessions. Economics is an important influence on the response of poor households. The studies of Sultana and Rayhan (2012) and Ninno *et al.* (2001) also reported that borrowing money was the most widely used coping strategy by flood-affected people. Another study found that local people in Tanzania reduce their numbers of meals and amount of consumption a day (Maxwell *et al.*,

1999). These findings are consistent with the results of the present study. Household coping strategies hence depend largely on the social and occupational structures of families and communities, as well as the physical setting of the family home in relation to the source of the water (Paul & Routray, 2009). These findings confirm the earlier proposition of Kunii *et al.* (2002) and Haque and Zaman (1993) that the flood problem in Bangladesh is not simply a physical hydraulic dynamic; it is also linked to issues of demography, education, settlement pattern, society, socio-economic status and even culture and politics. In the present study, flood-prone households on the Padma River islands do not find great value in centralized or technologically brokered flood warnings, but they save and borrow money, diversify their income sources and modify their homes as a preventive measure in the pre-disaster period. Moreover, they also adjust their behavior to utilize social structures to be more resilient, including drawing on the resources of friends and neighbours, and taking precautionary measures to protect their goods from damage within the household. The value of household level economic, social and technological coping strategies in combating the negative impacts of flood disasters contributes to the Sustainable Development Goals achievement literature, highlighting how disaster risk can be minimized by drawing on households' abilities.

Acknowledgements

We would like to thank the villagers from Narayanpur Mauza who participated in this research. We would like to express our gratitude to Professor Dr. Syed Rafiqul Alam Rumi and Professor Dr. Abu Hanif Shaikh, Rajshahi University. We thank the Ministry of Science and Technology, Bangladesh for funding this research.

References

Adger, W. N. (2006). Vulnerability. *Global Environmental Change, 16*(3), 268–281.
Adger, W. N., Huq, S., Brown, K., Conway, D., & Hulme, M. (2003). Adaptation to climate change in the developing world. *Progress Development Studies, 3*(3), 179–195.
Agrawala, S., Ota, T., Ahmed, A. U., Smith, J., & Aalst, M. V. (2003). *Development and Climate Change in Bangladesh: Focus on Coastal Flooding and the Sundarbans.* Report No.: COM/ENV/EPOC/DCD/DAC(2003)3/FINAL. OECD, Paris.
Alam, G. M. M., Alam, K., & Shahbaz, M. (2016). Influence of institutional access and social capital on adaptation choices: Empirical evidence from vulnerable rural households in Bangladesh. *Ecological Economics, 130*, 243–251.
Alam, G. M. M., Alam, K., Shahbaz, M., & Clarke, M. L. (2017). Drivers of vulnerability to climatic change in riparian char and river-bank households in Bangladesh: Implications for policy, livelihoods and social development. *Ecological Indicators, 72*, 23–32.

Benson, C., Twigg, J., & Myers, M. (2001). NGO initiatives in risk reduction: An overview. *Disasters, 25,* 199–215. DOI: 10.1111/1467–7717.00172

Blaikie, P. T., Cannon, I. D., & Wisner, B. (1994). *At Risk: Natural Hazards, People's Vulnerability, and Disasters.* London, UK: Routledge.

Bollin, C., & Hidajat, R. (2003). Community-based risk index: Pilot implementation in Indonesia. In J. Brikmann (Ed.), *Measuring Vulnerability to Natural Hazards: Towards Disaster. Resilient Societies* (pp. 271–289). Shibuya-ku, Tokyo: United Nations University Press.

Davis, S. (1996). *Adaptable Livelihoods: Coping with Food Insecurity in the Malian Sahel.* London, UK: Palgrave Macmillan.

Emrich, C. T., & Cutter, S. L. (2011). Social vulnerability to climate-sensitive hazards in the southern United States. *Weather, Climate, and Society, 3*(3), 193–208.

Fenton, A., Paavola, J., & Tallontire, A. (2017). Autonomous adaptation to riverine flooding in Satkhira District, Bangladesh: Implications for adaptation planning. *Regional Environmental Change, 17,* 2387–2396. DOI: 10.1007/s10113-017-1159-8

Few, R. (2003). Flooding, vulnerability and coping strategies: Local responses to a global threat. *Progress in Development Studies, 3*(1), 43–58.

Flood Forecasting & Warning Center. (2016). *Annual Flood Report,* Bangladesh Water Development Board.

Frankenberger, T. (1992). Indicators and data collection methods for assessing household food security. In S. Maxwell & T. Frankenberger (Eds.), *Household Food Security: Concepts, Indicators, and Measurements: A Technical Review.* New York, NY, USA and Rome: UNICEF and IFAD.

Gandure, S., Walker, S., & Botha, J. J. (2013). Farmers' perceptions of adaptation to climate change and water stress in a South Africal rural community. *Environmental Development, 5,* 39–53.

Government of Bangladesh. (1992). *Flood Modeling and Management, Flood Hydrology Study, Main Report.* Government of Bangladesh, Dhaka.

Government of Bangladesh. (2006). *Flood Forecasting and Warning Centre Report.* Dhaka, Bangladesh.

Handmer, J., Penning, E., & Tapsell, S. (1999). Flooding in a warmer world: The view from Europe. In T. E. Downing, A. A. Olsthoorn, & R. S. J. Tol (Eds.), *Climate, Change and Risk* (pp. 125–161). London, UK: Routledge.

Haque, C. E., & Zaman, M. Q. (1993). Human responses to riverine hazards in Bangladesh: A proposal for sustainable floodplain development. *World Development, 21*(1), 93–107.

Intergovernmental Panel on Climate Change (IPCC). 2013. *Climate Change 2013: Synthesis Report.* The Physical Science Basis, 5th Assessment Report. Cambridge, New York: Cambridge University Press.

Islam, A. K. M. S., Bala, S. K., Hussain, M. A., Hossain, M. A., & Rahman, M. (2011). Performance of coastal structures during cyclone Sidr. *Nature Hazards Review, 12*(2), 111–116.

Islam, M. A., Mitra, D., Dewan, A., & Akhter, S. H. (2016). Coastal multi-hazard vulnerability assessment along the Ganges deltaic coast of Bangladesh: A geospatial approach. *Ocean & Coastal Management, 127,* 1–15.

Islam, R., Walkerden, G., & Amati, M. (2017). Households' experience of local government during recovery from cyclones in coastal Bangladesh: Resilience, equity, and corruption. *Natural Hazards Review, 85*(1), 361–378.

Jonkman, S. N., & Kelman, I. (2005). An analysis of the causes and circumstances of flood disaster deaths. *Disasters, 29*(1), 75–97.

Jordan, J. C. (2015). Swimming alone? The role of social capital in enhancing local resilience to climate stress: A case study from Bangladesh. *Climate and Development, 7*(2), 110–123.

Kunii, O., Nakamura, S., Rahman, A., & Wakai, S. (2002). The impact on health and risk factors of the diarrhea epidemics in the 1998 Bangladesh floods. *Public Health, 116*(2), 68–74.

Mallick, B., Witte, S. M., Sarkar, R., Mahboob, A. S., & Vogt, J. (2009). Local adaptation strategies of a coastal community during cyclone Sidr and their vulnerability analysis for sustainable disaster mitigation planning in Bangladesh. *Journal of Bangladesh Institute of Planners, 2*, 158–168.

Maxwell, D., Ahaideke, C., Levin, C., Armar, M., Zakariah, S., & Lamptey, G. M. (1999). Alternative food security indicators: Revisiting the frequency and severity of coping strategies. *Food Policy, 24*, 411–429.

Mirza, Q. M. M. (2002). Global warming and changes in the probability of occurrence of floods in Bangladesh and implications. *Global Environmental Change, 12*(2), 127–138.

Mirza, Q. M. M., Warrick, R. A., Ericksen, N. J., & Kenny, G. J. (2001). Are floods getting worse in the Ganges, Brahmaputra and Meghna Basins? *Environmental Hazards, 3*(2), 37–48.

Niles, M. T., Lubell, M., & Brown, M. (2015). How limiting factors drive agricultural adaptation to climate change. *Agriculture Ecosystem and Environment, 200*, 178–185. https://doi.org/10.1016/j.agee.2014.11.010

Ninno, C. D., Dorosh, P. A., Smith, L. C., & Roy, D. K. (2001). The 1998 floods in Bangladesh: Disaster impacts, household coping strategies and response. *Research Report 122*. Washington, DC: IFPRI.

Osuret, J., Atuyambe, L. M., Mayega, R. W., Ssentongo, J., Tumuhamye, N., Mongo, B. G., . . . Bazeyo, W. (2016). Coping strategies for landslide and flood disasters: A qualitative study of Mt. Elgon Region, Uganda. In *Currents Disasters* (Edition 1). DOI: 10.1371/currents.dis.4250a225860babf3601a18e33e172d8b

Paul, B. K. (1997). Flood research in Bangladesh in retrospect and prospect: A review. *Geoforum, 28*(2), 121–131.

Paul, B. K. (2010). Human injuries caused by Bangladesh's cyclone Sidr: An empirical study. *Natural Hazards, 54*(2), 483–495.

Paul, S. K. (2012). Vulnerability to tropical cyclone in the southern Bangladesh: Impacts and determinants. *Oriental Geographer, 53*(1–2), 19–40.

Paul, S. K., & Routray, J. K. (2009). Flood proneness and coping strategies: The experiences of two villages in Bangladesh. *Disasters, 34*, 489–508. DOI: 10.1111/j.1467–7717.2009.01139.x

Rasid, H., & Paul, B. K. (1987). Flood problems in Bangladesh: Is there an indigenous solution. *Environmental Management, 11*(2), 155–173.

Smith, K. (1996). *Environmental Hazards: Assessing Risk and Reducing Disaster*. London, UK: Routledge.

Sultana, N., & Rayhan, M. I. (2012). Coping strategies with floods in Bangladesh: An empirical study. *Nature Hazards, 64*, 1209. http://sci-hub.tw/10.1007/s11069-012-0291-5

Sultana, R., & Alam, M. S. (2016). Island dwellers perceptions on Padma River flood. *International Journal of Advanced Research, 4*(11), 2447–2450. http://dx.doi.org/10.21474/IJAR01/2356

Sultana, R., Rumi, S. R. A., & Sheikh, A. H. (2013). Climate change induced flood risk and adaptation in the Padma River Island, Bangladesh: A local scale approach. *Journal of Life and Earth Science, 8*, 41–48. http://sci-hub.tw/10.3329/jles.v8i0.20138

Thompson, P., & Tod, I. (1998). Mitigating flood losses in the active floodplains of Bangladesh. *Disaster Prevention and Management, 7*(2), 113–123.

United States Agency for International Development (USAID). (1988). *OFDA Annual Report* (pp. 110–122). Office of the US Disaster Assistance Agency for International Development, Washington, DC.

Yamane, T. (1967). *Statistics: An Introductory Analysis*. New York, NY: Harper and Row.

Part 5

Sustainable Development Goal 14

Life below water

Sustainable Development Goal 15

Life on land

8 Meanings, opportunities and challenges of cultural ecosystem services-based coastal management in the Sundarbans mangroves, Bangladesh

Management priorities for achieving SDGs 14 and 15

Shamik Chakraborty, Shantanu Kumar Saha and Samiya Ahmed Selim

Introduction: meaning of cultural ecosystem services in respect to the Sundarbans

Marine and coastal ecosystems serve as vital life-supporting systems for coastal communities, especially in developing countries. It is estimated that more than 1 billion people depend on fish for animal protein, and about 300 million people depend on marine and coastal fisheries for their livelihoods (IIED, n.d.). The majority rely on small-scale, artisanal fisheries that are supported by traditional ecological knowledge (IIED n.d.; Mozumder *et al.*, 2018). Natural and semi-natural coastal ecosystems within the traditional ecological knowledge (TEK) pool play an essential role in human well-being and social and economic development worldwide; they are particularly crucial for local communities. Coastal ecosystems are hence increasingly recognized as socio-ecological systems as they have highly interlinked human and ecological components (Berkes *et al.*, 2003). Ecosystems that have these links can bring many ecosystem service benefits (that is, the material and non-material benefits that people obtain from nature), such as the provision of habitats, regulation of the balance of carbon dioxide from the atmosphere, protection of coastal areas from flooding and erosion, fisheries-based livelihoods and recreational and tourism opportunities; these are significant contributions to human well-being (Millennium Ecosystem Assessment [MA], 2005; Liquete *et al.*, 2013; Nunes & Gowdy, 2015). Recently concerns have been raised that a single, utilitarian approach to management can degrade many of these wider ecosystem services (Fisher & Brown, 2015). It is here that consideration of cultural ecosystem services (CES) can maintain coastal ecosystem services and their conservation from a non-utilitarian angle.

The Millennium Ecosystem Assessment (MA) refers to CES as aesthetic, spiritual, psychological and other non-material benefits that humans obtain from ecosystems (MA, 2005). CES are a vital part of ecosystem service-based approaches, and there is a need to raise managerial awareness (Spangenberg, 2014), particularly in marine and coastal settings where ecological and social systems are both highly connected and co-evolve at a range of spatial and temporal scales (Folke, 2006; Kikiloi, 2010; Hicks, 2011). Recent studies also suggest that CES can be bundled together with multiple ecosystem services such as provisioning (Klain *et al.*, 2014; Chan *et al.*, 2012). However the CES provided by coastal ecosystems are still not well conceptualized when compared to provisioning, regulating and supporting services (Rodrigues *et al.*, 2017). CES may be difficult to capture and study as they change with time, and they are also contested in nature (Milcu *et al.*, 2013; Plieninger *et al.*, 2015) between different resource users (Dzingirai & Bourdillon, 1997). There remains a lack of appropriate data for understanding CES, as well as a lack of information at local scales on the people who are benefitting from the flow of cultural services (Ambrose-Oji & Pagella, 2012). With the above premise, this chapter discusses the role of CES-based management in the Sundarbans mangrove ecosystem in Bangladesh.

The Sundarbans is the largest single tract of mangrove forest in the world, lying in the deltaic area of the Ganges and Brahmaputra Rivers on the Bay of Bengal, comprising a complex network of meandering tidal channels, low silt and clay islands and salt-tolerant bushy and tree vegetation – it is strikingly beautiful. Some 60% of the territory lies in the southwest region of Bangladesh, with the remainder in the West Bengal state of India (Figure 8.2). The Bangladeshi part has been a UNESCO World Heritage Site since 1997, with 140,000 hectares of the core area in three wildlife sanctuaries; it is the only World Heritage Site in Bangladesh based on natural ecosystem properties. The area is a biodiversity hotspot, and is home to some 453 animal species, 291 species of fish and 22 families of trees (Iftekhar & Islam, 2004; Iftekhar & Saenger, 2008). The Sundarbans is also famous for iconic species such as the royal Bengal tiger (*Panthera tigris*), mugger crocodile (*Crocodylus palustris*), river terrapin (*Batagur baska*), and Gangetic river dolphin (*Platanista gangetica*). The conservation of these animals requires a holistic appraisal of the physical-biological attributes of their habitats.

The Sundarbans is also a major economic asset. The estuarine mangrove ecosystem provides significant natural capital to the economy of Bangladesh, since more than 3.5 million people depend directly on its assets for their livelihoods (Giri *et al.*, 2007; Mozumder *et al.*, 2018). It is also a socio-ecological system that has evolved through biophysical and socio-cultural processes (Matin & Taylor, 2015); people have deep cultural attachments to the wild coastal mangrove forests, and the forest contributes significantly to their well-being. The Sundarbans provides subsistence-based livelihoods for wood-cutters, fishermen, honey gatherers and leaf and grass gatherers in surrounding villages. The mangrove trees and roots also act as a protective buffer from storm surges, seawater seepage and salinity intrusion along the coastline (Barbier, 2007; Walters *et al.*, 2008; Uddin *et al.*, 2013). In the following section, we elaborate further on the Sundarbans as a socio-ecological system, and its role in releasing a cluster of ecosystem services through cultural interactions.

Socio-ecological interactions through cultural ecosystem services in the Sundarbans

Since the early periods of resource planning in the eighteenth century, the Sundarbans has been managed in a strictly utilitarian way. From 1769, the mangroves were jointly managed by Indian and (later) Bangladeshi central authorities, and policies were established to try to achieve a sustained yield of forestry and fisheries resources available from these mangroves (Chowdhury & Ahmed, 1994; Choudhury, 1997). However, TEK and the cultural interaction with the mangroves did not attract serious attention when sustainable yields were being determined. In 1997, three wildlife sanctuaries (the East, West and South sanctuaries) were created to protect the natural heritage of this mangrove forest, and to protect its further deterioration due to the dwindling mangrove forest area (UNESCO, n.d.). However, according to Islam and Wahab (2005) these sanctuaries are small and fragmented to allow complete long-term wildlife conservation (Figure 8.1). Moreover, because of the proximity of the sea these three low-lying sanctuaries are expected to receive the full effect of any sea level rise, which will shrink the residual area of terrestrial ecosystems. Protection of mangroves outside the core reserve areas is therefore a necessity, even to maintain the areal extent of the sanctuaries.

With a background of further threats to the marine and coastal ecosystems from climate change, ocean acidification, water pollution and overfishing, a viable solution for maintaining TEK-based small-scale artisanal fisheries and forestry is required. Recently, scholars have put importance to these types of traditional management systems people have with the mangroves are put to importance (Queiroz *et al.*, 2017). This is especially true because of the ways in which fisheries have become commercialized around the

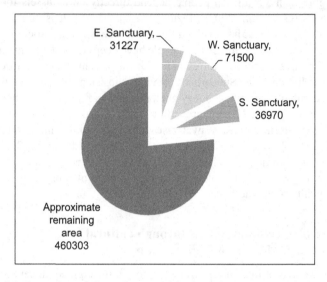

Figure 8.1 Comparison of the areal extent of the Sundarbans mangroves in Bangladesh (Numbers denote area in hectares)

world (Kroodsma *et al.*, 2018) and primary forest areas have been compromised by development (Lamb *et al.*, 2005). Without the central role played by culture in maintaining such ecosystems, human well-being can be seriously compromised, as vital and life-supporting ecosystem services can be traded off for exploitation of resources. TEK is a key aspect of utilizing biodiversity-related services in a sustainable way, and is increasingly seen as vital for ecosystem-based adaptive management. It also implies that TEK, with its links to ecosystem health, can lead to culturally appropriate adaptation (Girot *et al.*, 2012). The interlinked nature of coastal social ecological systems (SES) needs to be analyzed because coastal planning revolves around environmental and economic values and currently those values remain disconnected from socio-cultural values (Kenter, 2016).

With high input of TEK for harvesting forest resources, the Sundarbans mangrove ecosystem shows a highly interlinked characteristic between people (resource harvesters) and mangrove forests. However, this TEK is at the crossroads of complex and irreversible changes at multiple scales, and hence is difficult to comprehend. For example, at the local scale, the mangroves are affected by a greater number of outmigration of local and traditional communities in search for work that enables non-Indigenous people to move in the area and change the mangroves to unsustainable prawn cultivation (a major factor stated in our study). At a larger scale, climate change is suspected to have been reducing the numbers of two key tree species of the Sundarbans, *sundari* (*Heritiera fomes*) and *gewa* (*Excoecaria agallocha*); it remains unclear how reduction in these species will affect the mangrove ecosystems (Uddin *et al.*, 2013). Dams and barrages erected in the upstream of the Ganges river system (particularly, the Farakka barrage) are suspected to have dwindled the freshwater inflow needed to maintain the natural mangrove forests (UNESCO, n.d.).

Although the Sundarbans is managed as a World Heritage Site, the ecosystem is unlikely to be able to be maintained by 'command and control' and tourism-based interventions only. There are numerous socio-economic and political-ecological bottlenecks, such as poverty in the forest fringe communities and consequent friction with and breaching of laws by customary resource users, overlain with corruption at many levels (Rahman *et al.*, 2010). These make achieving sustainable management of the mangroves through top-down management interventions a challenging task, and it is here that an appreciation for cultural interactions with the mangroves is needed.

To comprehend the cultural linkages of the Sundarbans socio-ecological system, we adopted a narrative-based approach and interviewed twelve local resource harvesters from three villages in the Batiaghata (Debitala and Katianangla villages) and Dacope (Dangmari village) sub-districts of the Khulna district (Figure 8.2) in June 2017. The resource harvesters included fishermen, honey collectors and golpata (*Nypa fruticans*) collectors, the three most widespread practices utilizing TEK; the resources harvested provide wood, roofing materials, wax, honey, food and medicinal products. To explore their TEK, we questioned villagers on their methods of harvesting, and their perceptions and attitudes towards the mangroves. Two main types of questions were asked, namely (1) the characteristics of their resource harvesting and (2) how local harvesters continue their involvement in day-to-day activities while venturing into the forest, and whether recent changes have degraded their livelihoods. The data were analyzed through content analysis, and coded through open and axial coding (Bazeley, 2013). Different categories of information obtained from the open coding were grouped into specific themes (particularly diversity of ecosystem services and the challenges of mangrove maintenance) for axial coding, and ultimately for selective coding (Chakraborty, 2018), which in this case was concerned with the sustainability of the mangrove areas.

The responses suggest that *cultural* interactions through selective resource extraction, limited access and metaphors regarding tigers have enabled the

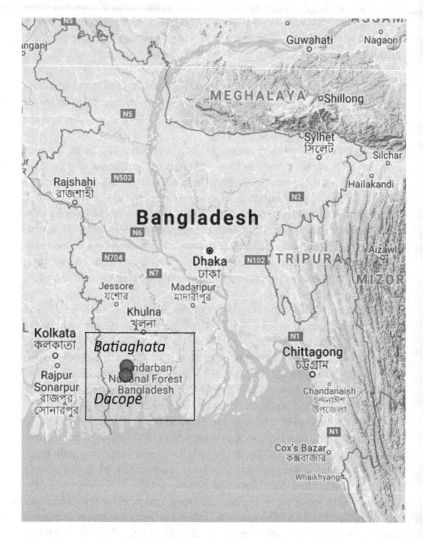

Figure 8.2 Location of the study area

maintenance of a bundle of ecosystem services (Table 8.1; Figure 8.3 and Figure 8.4). These three components work together, supported by TEK regarding resource harvesting, to bind the socio-ecological interlinkages of the Sundarbans. The selected ecosystem services related to these three main types of cultural linkages are shown in Table 8.2.

Table 8.1 Socio-ecological components of the Sundarbans mangroves

Three components of human-nature interlinkage in the Sundarbans socio-ecological system	Examples of interlinkages between TEK and natural elements	Sustainability components that maintain resources in the long term
Selective extractions	• Cut only the mid parts and older leaves of golpata so that the plant can regrow • Do not cut during growing periods • Prune stems that will not grow • Set fishing nets temporarily, so that fish are taken only during high tide • Retain about two-thirds of the beehive so that bees can recolonize the same hive • Avoid killing young bees during honey collection • Avoid fishing during the spawning season, and avoid catching fish larvae, fry and fingerlings • Use bag nets and stake nets	• Selective cutting, and low input artisanal fishing synchronized with the flow of tides • Reduce discards of bycatch • Recognize the importance of *goran, gewa, kholse, keora, baen and poshur*[1] niches as storehouses for wild honey • Maintain golpata niches that are used by tigers for resting and stalking
Limited access	• Special knowledge and mental maps of routes inside forests, including entries and exits • Follow bees to locate beehives deep inside the forest • Brave the fear of tigers inside the forest to allow any type of resource harvesting	• Knowledge about the tidal inflow and outflow of rivers and creeks • Knowledge about forest niches • Knowledge about bees and their movements inside the forest
Metaphors	• Belief that the tigers are the true protectors of the forest, sent to take out people who sin in the forests or do not obey the laws of the forest	• Animals rather than humans as the principal protector of ecosystems

Source: Field data by the authors

Tigers are accepted by villagers as apex predators within the Sundarbans ecosystem but are also viewed as sacred animals related to the forest gods *Bonbibi* and *Dakshinray*, the protectors of the mangroves. As the overarching species giving protection to wider species and habitats, the tiger is also understood through the metaphors present in the landscape. These metaphors predate modern scientific explanation of tigers as an important element of

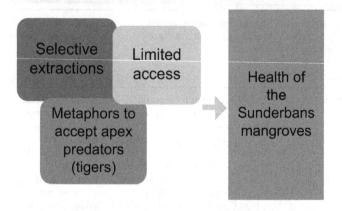

Figure 8.3 Three salient features of Sundarbans SES and their resilience

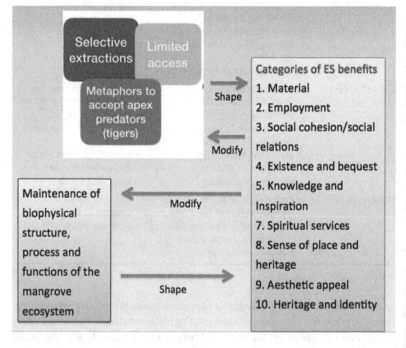

Figure 8.4 The relationship of three salient features of TEK and their relation to Sundarbans ecosystem benefits that are embedded within the larger sphere of biophysical structure, processes and functions of ecosystems

the local ecology, and remain a vital form of feedback for the Sundarbans socio-ecological system by maintaining the forest's health through *exclusion* of humans from the forest domain. This feedback also remains a key to human-(large) carnivore co-existence, a key factor for sustainable resource harvesting from forests in the Sundarbans.

However, this feedback is in peril because of the near extinction of tigers in the Sundarbans. A recent study using photography and more accurate camera footage-based methods of counting tigers suggests that, contrary to previous (pawprint-based) tiger census estimates of about 440 individuals, there may only be about 100 tigers left in the Bangladesh part of the Sundarbans (The Guardian, 2015). Although World Heritage status and eco-tourism opportunities could be a key to conserving the remaining tiger habitats, such 'new' interventions need to align with TEK and the communities that maintain this knowledge. It is particularly crucial to protect the mangroves over a larger area than covered by the three sanctuaries. It is here that we find a much-needed research priority, on how the three major socio-ecological components noted above, and the ecosystem services they support, are related to the larger sphere of the physical-biological structure, processes and functions of the Sundarbans mangroves. This understanding will help to achieve a fuller appreciation of the underlying ecological system that continuously shapes and is shaped by the type and quality of ecosystem services (Figure 8.4).

Since becoming a World Heritage Site, the increase in visitor numbers has raised recreational and tourism-related benefits in the minds of local people. Specifically, conservation awareness has become more widespread amongst the general population, not only amongst the traditional resource harvesters. This is a major departure from past practices and attitudes towards the value of the Sundarbans mangroves. Well-disposed individuals also help the government as they inform the forest office about illegal extraction of timber and wildlife, using mobile telephones (a facility enhanced by increasing the number of mobile phone users in the villages). Previously, local people often used to kill tigers that ventured inside their villages, but currently there are more incidents where villagers alert the local forest offices to relocate individuals back into the forest, despite knowing that the animal may venture in again, since the tiger's territory may not be far from the settlement.

Challenges for management of TEK

Faced with strong pressure from a growing population, and a relatively weak socio-economic and political background of conservation in the Sundarbans, World Heritage Site-based protection measures are certainly a positive management intervention. However, the challenges to securing long-term ecological benefits by protecting the mangroves remain cause for serious concern. Our study respondents mentioned that illegal and damaging resource harvesting from the core areas of the Sundarbans still takes place, regardless of the existence of strict protective measures. If traditional harvesting were allowed, minor non-compliance with the protected area laws would be less damaging to the health of the mangroves in comparison with non-traditional methods of securing resources.

TEK in the Sunderbans is threatened by different drivers of change, some of which are related to the degradation of the mangrove forests (indirect effects), while others are related to the degradation of the resource harvesters' socio-economic situation (direct effects). Currently, most tourist visits take place within the three protected areas, so the other parts of the forest, particularly the areas that are outside the protected areas, remain vulnerable to a range of illegal practices. Illegal logging for valuable *sundari* trees (*Heritiera fomes*), poaching of tigers and expansion of cultured shrimp and fisheries (a major concern expressed by the local resource harvesters during group discussions), pollution (including oil spills) from the increasingly industrialized coastal areas upstream, forest fires, destructive salt making and overgrazing have been noted. Moreover, top dying disease of the *sundari* trees (*H. fomes*) has recently been found. Although no definitive cause for this has been identified, it is thought to be the result of stress to the trees associated with human-induced heavy metal contamination of the sediment deposited on the islands and in the channels. These findings are in agreement with common anthropogenic pressures noted by other studies as well (Iftekhar & Islam, 2004; Iftekhar, 2004; FAO, 2000; Rahman *et al.*, 2009, 2010). These indirectly have an adverse effect on the local TEK pool associated with resource harvesting from the mangrove forests. TEK is also threatened indirectly by the changing forest structure both due to climatic change and other external changes, for example by development projects such as Rampal Power Plant[2] and poor resource management (Giri *et al.*, 2007). Other specific concerns expressed by the mangrove resource harvesters include littering and excessive numbers of tourist launches in the rivers such that they disturb the wildlife and encroach on the hunting and foraging territory of native wild animals.

The major concern of the traditional resource harvesters is that they personally, and their valuable pool of TEK, are vulnerable to a vicious cycle of money lending, bribery and corruption; this clogs the socio-cultural elements of maintaining knowledge amongst the community (and thus, has a more direct effect on the degradation of the TEK pool). In fact, the greatest fear of the local resource harvesters is no longer tigers, but bandits who repeatedly kidnap resource harvesters and demand ransom money from their families and friends. In order to pay the ransoms, the resource harvesters turn to the money lenders and the 'debt' is never paid back. Some non-traditional resource harvesters also try to acquire more fish or other produce than traditional sustainable methods would allow, sometimes by poisoning upstream creeks or clear felling nypa palms (*Nypa fructis*) or cutting wood illegally from the forests, disregarding traditional methods of husbandry.

Cultural interlinkage as a new opportunity for ICZM in order to achieve SDG 14 and 15 in Bangladesh

The 17 United Nations Sustainable Development Goals (SDGs) with their embedded total of 169 targets are expected to aid the transition towards sustainable resource use of our oceans, seas and forests. Specifically, biodiversity and conservation of ecosystems form the basis of SGDs 14 and 15, and their contribution to ecosystem services and human well-being underpins the achievement of all the other goals (Wood *et al.*, 2018). SDG 14 refers to the conservation and sustainable use of oceans, seas and marine resources, whereas SDG 15 makes reference to protection, restoration and sustainable use of terrestrial ecosystems. SDG 15 refers specifically to sustainable management of forests, halting and reversing land degradation and halting biodiversity loss. The management of the Sundarbans ecosystems is very much required for achieving SDGs 14 and 15. These Goals also provide scope for applying novel ideas and notions to cope with unsustainable coastal resource utilization. It is therefore appropriate that some of the inventive social solutions embedded in TEK be addressed and analyzed to help maintain the value and diversity of coastal ecosystems.

The present status of Bangladesh's coastal mangrove ecosystem and the resources within them reflect a lack of significant ecosystem restoration efforts, data collection and analysis that lacks rigour and standardization, management decisions (such as definitions of 'allowable' catches) that are based on weak science and poor understanding of the TEK and lack of understanding of the regulations on marine resources for small-scale artisanal fishers (Mozumder, *et al.*, 2018). For Bangladesh, these are all pressing issues that need to be considered when developing policies and strategies to achieve SDGs 14 and 15. The linkages of different ecosystem services available from cultural interactions with the natural environments of the Sundarbans to the specific targets of SDG 14 and 15 are described in Table 8.2 below.

'Integrated Coastal Zone Management' (ICZM) represents a dynamic and continuous process that has broadened the scope of sustainable management of coastal areas in Europe and elsewhere, and could be brought to bear in this Bangladeshi context. (European Commission, 1999). The TEK of Indigenous and local communities should be pursued as a major part of

Table 8.2 Selected ecosystem services from the mangroves and their definitions as understood in our study

Ecosystem services available in the study area	Examples	Links to targets in SDGs 14 and 15
Material	Wax, honey, fish, nypa palm, on a subsistence basis	14.1, 14.2, 14.4, 14.B, 15.1, 15.2, 15.5, 15.9
Employment	Employed in direct acquisition of mangrove resources through traditional methods	14.4, 14.B, 15.1, 15.9
Social cohesion/social relations	Storytelling and group-based learning through direct observation, that binds the forest dweller society together	14.2, 15.2, 15.5, 15.9
Existence and bequest	'No forest – no life' perception of the forest resource harvesters	14.B 15.5, 15.9, 15.C
Knowledge and inspiration	Experience-based TEK gathered through interaction with the mangrove ecosystem, and storytelling about individuals' experiences as inspirations to visit the forests	14.B 15.5, 15.9, 15.B
Spiritual services	Metaphors that the Sundarbans mangroves are protected by *dakshinray*; the souls of the people are protected by the cult of *bonobibi*	14.2, 15.9, 15.B, 15.C
Sense of place and heritage	Cultural attachment of different forest niches, rivers and creeks to livelihoods; existence of sacred temples of *bonobibi* inside the forest	14.2, 14.4 15.2, 15.5, 15.9
Aesthetic appeal	Mangrove forests with particular aesthetic beauty, especially those outside the normal touristic destinations	14.5 15.2, 15.5, 15.7, 15.9
Heritage and identity	Groups of fishermen, honey collectors and golpata collectors brought together through common beliefs and practices	14.2, 14.4, 14.7 15.B, 15.C

Source: Field data by the authors and following websites: https://sustainabledevelopment.un.org/sdg14, https://sustainabledevelopment.un.org/sdg15

the ICZM process in Bangladesh. ICZM has also emerged as an interactive planning process capable of dealing with complex issues (Thia-Eng, 1993). More recent coastal management policies in Bangladesh can be complementary to the overall goals of ICZM. For example, Bangladesh's Coastal Zone

Policy of 2005 could be a vehicle for implementation of ICZM, including utilizing TEK to capture a fuller spectrum of coastal socio-ecological systems. Such integrated management scenarios create a major opportunity to apply participatory, community-based and interdisciplinary approaches for holistic management. Local community stakeholders can become day-to-day managers of their local resources, and stakeholders with better awareness of TEK can better realize ICZM. Application of such a 'bottom-up' policy generates better understanding of the interlinkages and status of the TEK pool present in and around the Sundarbans mangroves. It also assists in overcoming implementation bottlenecks to traditionally based resource use practices on the ground. Recognition of the TEK pools is a necessity for relevant, stronger and well-defined legal frameworks; based on the evidence of our field study, the TEK pools do not currently have a strong legal status. Inclusive participation – including participation of the political actors – is an urgent necessity for effective collaboration and better utilization of human resources.

Conclusion

Termed 'rainforests of the seas', major mangrove zones such as the Sundarbans provide critical habitat-support functions for both terrestrial and marine biological diversity. Based on our research with local communities, we provide three salient points to note in conclusion. These are:

1   Cultural ecological systems of the Sundarbans mangrove ecosystem should be a salient part of integrated coastal zone management in Bangladesh, as the country tries to implement ecosystem-based, adaptive coastal ecosystem management based on multiple uses.

(Van Lavieren *et al.*, 2012)

2   Successful mangrove conservation and restoration to realize Sustainable Development Goals 14 and 15 will require blending of natural environmental and socio-economic components, incorporating both the science of ecosystem dynamics, and TEK. Cultural ecosystem services open up an opportunity to mobilize these two types of knowledge at the landscape level.

3   In our case, selective extractions, metaphors to accept tigers as an apex predator and the true protector of the forests and limited access are the three overarching socio-ecological components that are related to a bundle of ecosystem services acquired by the locals (e.g., the flow of ecosystem services have a strong cultural component). These socio-ecological components are related to maintenance of a number of ecosystem services and to multiple targets of SDGs 14 and 15.

Based on these findings, we recommend more systematic study of TEK pools in the Sundarbans, alongside exploration of how this knowledge can be mainstreamed into local- and national-level policies and decision-making regarding sustainable management of the mangrove ecosystems.

Notes

1 Goran (*Ceriops decandra*), gewa (*Excoecaria agallocha*), kholse (*Aegiceras corniculatum*), keora (*Sonneratia apetala*), baen (*Avicennia*) and poshur (*Xylocarpus mekongensis*).
2 The Rampal coal-fired power plant is a controversial venture that potentially violates World Heritage status by being sited just 14 km upstream from the Sundarbans (within 25 km of the protected area). When in operation, the project is expected to cause serious ecological harm to the Sundarbans through pollution and adverse impacts on aquatic and terrestrial habitats (The Guardian, 2016).

References

Ambrose-Oji, B., & Pagella, T. (2012). *Spatial Analysis and Prioritisation of Cultural Ecosystem Services: A Review of Methods* (Research Report, Forest Research). Surrey: Alice Holt Lodge Farnham. Retrieved from https://forestry.gov.uk/pdf/CES_spatial_analysis_tools_review_2102.pdf/$FILE/CES_spatial_analysis_tools_review_2102.pdf

Barbier, E. B. (2007). Valuing ecosystem services as productive inputs. *Economic Policy, 22*(49), 178–229.

Bazeley, P. (2013). *Qualitative Data Analysis: Practical Strategies*. London: Sage.

Berkes, F., Colding, J., & Folke, C. (2003). *Navigating Social: Ecological Systems: Building Resilience for Complexity and Change*. Cambridge, UK: Cambridge University Press.

Chakraborty, A. (2018). Challenges for environmental sustainability in a mountain destination: Insights from the Shiroumadake District of North Japan Alps. *Geo-Journal*, 1–21. https://doi.org/10.1007/s10708-018-9868-1

Chan, K., Goldstein, J., Satterfield, T., Hannahs, N., Kikiloi, K., Naidoo, R., . . . Woodside, U. (2012). Cultural services and non-use values. In P. Kareiva, H. Tallis, T. H. Ricketts, G. C. Daily, & S. Polasky (Eds.), *Natural Capital: Theory and Practice of Mapping Ecosystem Services* (pp. 206–228). Oxford, UK: Oxford University Press.

Choudhury, J. K. (1997). *Sustainable management of coastal mangrove forest development and social needs*. Proceedings of the XI World Forestry Congress, Vol. 6, topic 38.6.

Chowdhury, R. A., & Ahmed, I. (1994). History of forest management Bangladesh. In Z. Hussain & G. Acharya (Eds.), *Mangroves of the Sundarbans* (pp. 155–180). Bangkok, Thailand: IUCN Wetlands Program, Gland.

Dzingirai, V., & Bourdillon, M. F. C. (1997). Religious ritual and political control in Binga District, Zimbabwe. *African Anthropology, 4*(2), 4–26.

European Commission. (1999). *Towards a European Integrated Coastal Zone Management (ICZM) Strategy: General Principles and Policy Options.* A Reflection Paper. The European Communities, Luxemburg. Retrieved from http://ec.europa. eu/environment/iczm/pdf/vol1.pdf

Fisher, J. A., & Brown, K. (2015). Reprint of "Ecosystem services concepts and approaches in conservation: Just a rhetorical tool?" *Ecological Economics, 117,* 261–269. https://doi.org/10.1016/j.ecolecon.2014.12.009

Folke, C. (2006). Resilience: The emergence of a perspective for social-ecological systems analyses. *Global Environmental Change, 16*(3), 253–267.

Food and Agriculture Organization. (2000). *State of World's Forests 2003.* Rome, Italy: FAO.

Giri, C., Pengra, B., Zhu, Z., Singh, A., & Tieszen, L. L. (2007). Monitoring mangrove forest dynamics of the Sundarbans in Bangladesh and India using multitemporal satellite data from 1973 to 2000. *Estuarine, Coastal and Shelf Science, 73,* 91–100.

Girot, P., Ehrhart, C., Oglethorpe, J., Reid, H., Rossing, T., Gambarelli, G., & Phillips, J. (2012). *Integrating community and ecosystem-based approaches in climate change adaptation responses.* ELAN, unpublished. Retrieved from www.elanadapt.net

The Guardian. (2015). Only 100 tigers left in Bangladesh's famed Sundarbans forest. Retrieved on 2018.03.02 from www.theguardian.com/environment/2015/jul/27/only-100-tigers-left-in-bangladeshs-famed-sundarbans-forest

The Guardian. (2016). UN tells Bangladesh to halt mangrove-threatening coal plant. Retrieved on 2018.03.02 from www.theguardian.com/environment/2016/oct/19/un-tells-bangladesh-to-halt-mangrove-threatening-coal-plant

Hicks, C. C. (2011). How do we value our reefs? Risks and tradeoffs across scales in "biomass-based" economies. *Coastal Management, 39*(4), 358–376.

Iftekhar, M. S. (2004). Environmental consciences of oil pollution on the Bangladesh Sundarban: A brief review. *ISME, 3,* 11.

Iftekhar, M. S., & Islam, M. R. (2004). Managing mangroves in Bangladesh: A strategy analysis. *Journal of Coastal Conservation, 10*(1), 139–146.

Iftekhar, M. S., & Saenger, P. (2008). Vegetation dynamics in the Bangladesh Sundarbans mangroves: A review of forest inventories. *Wetlands Ecology and Management, 16*(4), 291–312.

International Institute for Environment and Development. (n.d.). *Ocean and Fisheries Economics.* Retrieved on 2018.03.21 from http://pubs.iied.org/pdfs/G04027.pdf

Islam, M. S., & Wahab, M. A. (2005). A review on the present status and management of mangrove wetland habitat resources in Bangladesh with emphasis on mangrove fisheries and aquaculture. *Hydrobiologia, 542,* 165–190.

Kenter, J. O. (2016). Shared, plural and cultural values. *Ecosystem Services, 21B,* 175–372.

Kikiloi, K. (2010). Rebirth of an archipelago: Sustaining a Hawaiian cultural identity for people and homeland. *Hulili: Multidisplinary Research on Hawaiian Well-Being, 6,* 73–114.

Klain, S. C., Satterfield, T. A., & Chan, K. M. (2014). What matters and why? Ecosystem services and their bundled qualities. *Ecological Economics, 107,* 310–320.

Kroodsma, D. A., Mayorga, J., Hochberg, T., Miller, N. A., Boerder, K., Ferretti, F., . . . Woods, P. (2018). Tracking the global footprint of fisheries. *Science, 359*(6378), 904–908.

Lamb, D., Erskine, P. D., & Parrotta, J. A. (2005). Restoration of degraded tropical forest landscapes. *Science, 310*(5754), 1628–1632. https://doi.org/10.1126/science.1111773

Liquete, C., Piroddi, C., Drakou, E. G., Gurney, L., Katsanevakis, S., Charef, A., & Egoh, B. (2013). Current status and future prospects for the assessment of marine and coastal ecosystem services: A systematic review. *PLoS One, 8*(7), e67737. https://doi.org/10.1371/journal.pone.0067737

Matin, N., & Taylor, R. (2015). Emergence of human resilience in coastal ecosystems under environmental change. *Ecology and Society, 20*(2). https://doi.org/10.5751/ES-07321-200243

Milcu, A. L., Hanspach, J., & Fischer, J. (2013). Cultural ecosystem services: A literature review and prospects for future research. *Ecology and Society, 18*(3), 44. DOI: 10.5751/ES-05790–180344

Millennium Ecosystem Assessment. (2005). *Ecosystems and Human Well-Being: Synthesis.* Washington, DC: Island Press.

Mozumder, M. M. H., Shamsuzzaman, M. M., Nabi, M. R., & Karim, E. (2018). Social-ecological dynamics of the small scale fisheries in Sundarban Mangrove Forest, Bangladesh. *Aqcuaculture and Fisheries, 3*(1), 38–49.

Nunes, P. A. L. D., & Gowdy, J. (2015). Marine economics and policy related to ecosystem services: Lessons from the world's regional seas. *Ecosystem Services, 11*, 1–148.

Plieninger, T., Bieling, C., Fagerholm, N., Byg, A., Hartel, T., Hurley, P., . . . Van Der Horst, D. (2015). *Current Opinion in Environmental Sustainability, 14*, 28–33.

Queiroz, L. de S., Rossi, S., Calvet-Mir, L., Ruiz-Mallén, I., García-Betorz, S., Salvà-Prat, J., & Meireles, A. J. de A. (2017). Neglected ecosystem services: Highlighting the socio-cultural perception of mangroves in decision-making processes. *Ecosystem Services, 26*, 137–145. https://doi.org/10.1016/j.ecoser.2017.06.013

Rahman, M. M., Chongling, Y., Islam, K. S., & Haoliang, L. (2009). A brief review on pollution and ecotoxicologic effect on Sundarbans mangrove ecosystem in Bangladesh. *International Journal of Environmental Engineering, 1*, 369–382.

Rahman, M. M., Rahman, M. M., & Islam, K. S. (2010). The causes of deterioration of Sundarban mangrove forest ecosystem of Bangladesh: Conservation and sustainable management issues. *AACL Bioflux, 2*(3), 77–90.

Rodrigues, J. G., Conides, A. J., Rodriguez, S. R., Raicevich, S., Pita, P., Kleisner, K. M., . . . Villasant, S. (2017). Marine and coastal cultural ecosystem services: Knowledge gaps and research priorities. *One Ecosystem, 2*, e12290. https://doi.org/10.3897/oneeco.2.e12290

Spangenberg, J. H. (2014). Ecosystem service in a social context. In S. Jacobs, N. Dendonker, & H. Keune (Eds.), *Ecosystem Services: Global Issues, Local Practices* (pp. 91–95). Amsterdam: Elsevier.

Thia-Eng, C. (1993). Essential elements of integrated coastal zone management. *Ocean & Coastal Management, 21*, 81–108.

Uddin, M. S., Shah, M. A. R., Khanom, S., & Nesha, M. K. (2013). Climate change impacts on the Sundarbans mangrove ecosystem services and dependent livelihoods in Bangladesh. *Asian Journal of Conservation Biology, 2*(2), 152–156.

Uddin, M. S., van Steveninck, E. D. R., Stuip, M., & Shah, M. A. R. (2013). Economic valuation of provisioning and cultural services of a protected mangrove ecosystem: A case study on Sundarbans Reserve Forest, Bangladesh. *Ecosystem Services, 5*, 88–93.

UNESCO. (n.d.). *Sundarban Wildlife Sanctuaries (Bangladesh)*. World Heritage Nomination – IUCN Technical Evaluation. Retrieved from https://whc.unesco.org/document/154300

Van Lavieren, H., Spalding, M., Alongi, D., Kainuma, M., Clüsener-Godt, M., & Adeel, Z. (Eds.). (2012). Securing the future of mangroves: A policy brief. *UNU-INWEH, UNESCO-MAB with ISME, ITTO, FAO, UNEP-WCMC and TNC* (pp. 1–53). United Nations University – Institute for Water, Environment and Health (UNU-INWEH).

Walters, B. B., Rönnbäck, P., Kovacs, J. M., Crona, B., Hussain, S. A., Badola, R., . . . Dahdouh-Guebas, F. (2008). Ethnobiology, socio-economics and management of mangrove forests: A review. *Aquatic Botany, 89*(2), 220–236.

Wood, S. L. R., Jones, S. K., Johnson, J. A., Brauman, K. A., Chaplin-Kramer, R., Fremier, A., . . . DeClerck, F. A. (2018). Distilling the role of ecosystem services in the Sustainable Development Goals. *Ecosystem Services, 29*, 70–82. https://doi.org/10.1016/j.ecoser.2017.10.010

Websites visited

https://sustainabledevelopment.un.org/sdg14
https://sustainabledevelopment.un.org/sdg15

9 Assessment of ecosystem service value in southwest coastal Bangladesh

Md. Wahidur Rahman Khan,
Md. Ali Akber, Md. Atikul Islam,
Md. Munsur Rahman and
Mohammad Rezaur Rahman

Introduction

The geographical region of the southwestern part of Bangladesh is unique in many ways. The presence of the largest mangrove forest of the world, the Sundarbans, and the distributaries of the Ganges, Hooghly, Padma, Brahmaputra and Meghna Rivers have together made this area rich in natural resources. A large but generally poor population depends directly or indirectly on the benefits or services provided by the mangrove forest ecosystem for their livelihoods. These services are known as 'ecosystem services'. Though these services are not fully recognized by human societies, ecosystem service valuation has been a hot topic in ecological economic research. Internationally, ecosystem service valuation has been widely linked to policies for improved water and living resources management, which promote conservation and at the same time foster human well-being (Pandeya *et al.*, 2016). Several studies over the past two decades have tried to estimate the values of a variety of ecosystem services. Kreuter *et al.* (2001) estimated temporal changes in ecosystem service values in the San Antonio area of Texas, USA. Konarska *et al.* (2002) evaluated the scale dependence of ecosystem service valuation, comparing NOAA-AVHRR and Landsat TM datasets. Zhao *et al.* (2004) assessed the ecosystem service value of land use change on Chongming Island and Tianhong *et al.* (2010) identified variations in ecosystem service value in response to shifts in land use in Shenzhen, both areas of China. Chen *et al.* (2013) determined the value of the ecosystem services in the Sanjiang plain, also in China, with Mendoza-González *et al.* (2014) providing an equivalent analysis for the Gulf of Mexico. More locally around the Bay of Bengal, Islam *et al.* (2014) identified the implications of agricultural land use change from 1980 to 2008, and observed that agricultural land reduced around 50%, whereas the shrimp farming increased around 50% within this time period. This indicates the major land use change pattern in southwest Bangladesh.

The study also discussed the negative impacts of this land use change on ecosystem services of the Ganges delta in Bangladesh. Khan *et al.* (2014) identified the relation between natural disasters and land use/land cover change of southwest coastal Bangladesh. The ecosystem service values determined by Costanza *et al.* (1997), and associated estimation of change in their global value (2014), were the most remarkable as pioneering work to place a monetary value on the world's 'ecosystem services and natural capital'. The study concluded that the annual net worth of the biosphere totals US$33 trillion, which is greater than the Gross National Products (GNP) of all the world's economies combined.

In the present study, land use valuation techniques have been used to identify current land use practices and to determine their ecosystem services values. This approach involves determining individual land use patterns and then using their value coefficients to determine the total value of the ecosystem services they provide to society. Landsat images from 2015 and a combined remote sensing and geographic information system (GIS) were used to determine land use practices and their associated areas of coverage. Previously published value coefficients from Costanza *et al.* (2014) for identical land uses in the Bay of Bengal were used to determine ecosystem services of the different areas.

One of the United Nations Sustainable Development Goals is to 'protect, restore and promote sustainable use of terrestrial ecosystems, sustainably manage forests, combat desertification, and halt and reverse land degradation and halt biodiversity loss'. Understanding the value of ecosystem services is of immense importance when taking initiatives towards promoting balanced and sustainable use of coastal terrestrial ecosystems, as it underpins choices about efforts to reinstate productive and sustainable food production, balanced against the wider ecological benefits of different types of land use. Hence the outcomes of this study will contribute to the sustainable development of coastal Bangladesh.

Materials and methods

Study area

The southwest coastal region of Bangladesh (between 21°39′N to 23°05′N and 88°54′E to 90°00′E) forms part of Ganges delta and is situated just north of the Bay of Bengal. The study area includes three districts of this region – Khulna, Satkhira and Bagerhat, covering a total of some 1,207 km². This area experiences tropical monsoon climatic conditions (hot and humid weather with abundant rainfall and seasonal variation). The humid summer stretches from March to May, a rainy season from June to September and a dry season from October to February. The Sundarbans, which is the largest mangrove forest of the world, lies in the southern part of the study area. It is a reserved forest and UNESCO declared Sundarbans a World Heritage Site in 1997, because of its ecological assets and beauty. Economically, the study area alone produces almost 80% of the total shrimp catch of Bangladesh, which in turn contributes about 9% of national exports earnings (Akber *et al.*, 2017). The

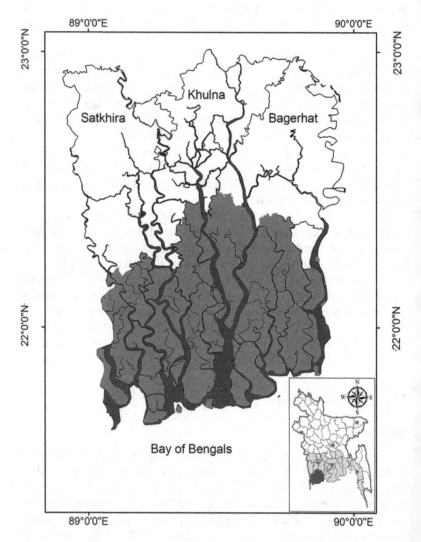

Figure 9.1 Location of the study area

location of the study area is illustrated in Figure 9.1. The southwest coastal area of Bangladesh was chosen for this study due to the existing rapid land use change and presence of unique ecosystem structure of this area. Extensive shrimp cultivated in this region is a major land use and environmental concern; however, shrimp is also a major export-earning sector of the country and important from the livelihood perspective of the local population. We confined the study area to three coastal districts – Satkhira, Khulna and Bagerhat – as they comprise the entire area of the southwest coast of Bangladesh.

Land use classification

Local data (historical maps, census statistics or commercial records) regarding land use practice were not available, so 2015 satellite images were used to determine land use types. Satellite images were downloaded from the United States Geological Survey webpages (www.earthexplorer.usgs.gov). In monsoonal areas, clouds frequently limit the use of satellite images and make it difficult to analyze the surface, so dry season images (December to January) were used to obtain cloud-free data. Images of four tiles were required: Path 137, Rows 44 and 45; Path 138, Rows 44 and 45.

Land use classification determination is a step-by-step process comprising image pre-processing, image mosaicking, image sub-setting, sample set preservation and supervised classification. Environment for Visualizing Images (ENVI 5.3) software was used to process the satellite images. Reflectance correction and dark subtraction tools were used for atmospheric correction, followed by a seamless mosaic tool to assemble the corrected images. The mosaic image covered the whole study area, but contained some extraneous areas, therefore a sub map was created that contained only the study area.

Five different land use practices were identified in southwest coastal Bangladesh: (1) agriculture (mainly paddies, but also some other crops like vegetable, fruits, lentils) (2) forest, (3) 'gher' or artificially constructed freshwater shrimp ponds, sometimes with other cultivated fish included, (4) river and (5) settlements and others. Different spectral responses were used for different land use practices, to generate regions of interest (ROI) using published band combinations. Finally, maximum likelihood algorithms were used under a supervised classification tool for land use classification. In this study, 'agricultural land' includes croplands, fallow lands, pastures, vegetation and canopies. 'Forest' includes the main Sundarbans wooded area, undifferentiated. 'River' includes river itself, whilst 'gher' includes all of the remaining surface water bodies excluding the river. 'Settlements' includes identifiable rural and urban areas, and other exposed lands mainly lacking vegetation and road networks.

Valuation of ecosystem services

To determine the ecosystem services of the study area, five land use practices were compared with the 16 biomes determined by Costanza *et al.*'s (2014) ecosystem service valuation model. The most similar biome was used as the proxy for specific local practice in the study area, namely, the 'cropland' biome for agricultural land, 'tidal marsh/mangrove' for Forest, 'lakes/rivers' biome for river and 'urban' for settlements and others as appropriate. There is no perfect proxy match for 'gher' in Costanza's valuation method. In theory, the wetland biome is somewhat similar; however, unlike wetlands, 'gher' ponds do not usually supply significant freshwater, regulate water flow, treat polluted water or have much recreational or cultural value. Food production was therefore considered the only ecosystem service offered by 'gher'. Table 9.1 represents the land use categories, equivalent biomes and ecosystem service coefficients.

Once the area of individual land use practice and its value coefficients had been determined, the following equation was used to determine individual ecosystem service:

$$ESV = \sum \left(A_k \times v_{Ck} \right) \tag{1.1}$$

Here ESV represents ecosystem service value, A_k is the area (ha) and v_{Ck} the value coefficient ($/ha/year) for land use category 'k'. The summation of the individual ecosystem services represents total ecosystem service for a specific year.

It is recognized that the use of different biomes as proxy in the valuation technique, especially in the case of 'gher', could lead to inaccuracies; over- or under-estimation of the ecosystem services offered by 'gher' could hence affect the total ecosystem service of the study area very significantly. Due to this potential unrepresentativeness, a coefficient of sensitivity was

Table 9.1 Land use practice, their equivalent biomes in Costanza *et al.* (2014) and the corresponding ecosystem service values

Land use practice	Equivalent biome	Ecosystem service coefficient ($ ha−1 per year)
Agricultural land	Cropland	5567
Forest	Mangrove	193,843
Gher	Wetlands	952
River	Rivers/lakes	12,512
Settlements and others	Urban	6661

analyzed using the standard economic concept of elasticity, that is, the percentage change in the output for a given percentage change in an input. The ecosystem value coefficients for agricultural land, forest, 'gher', river and settlements were each adjusted by ±50%. Though agricultural land, forest and rivers match the proxies of Costanza *et al.*'s (2014) biome, coefficients of sensitivity were calculated to find out their robustness.

$$CS = \frac{\left(ESV_j - ESV_i\right) / ESV_i}{\left(vC_{jk} - vC_{ik}\right) / vC_{ik}} \tag{1.2}$$

Coefficient of sensitivity (CS) represents the ratio of the percentage change in estimated total ecosystem value (ESV) and the percentage change in the adjusted valuation coefficient (vC). If the ratio is less than one, it indicates that the estimation of ecosystem service is robust, and if the ratio is greater than one, the estimation is elastic.

Results

Figure 9.2 illustrates the five land use practices in the southwest coastal area of Bangladesh. The overall accuracy of the classification has been determined by using ground truthing, knowledge-based judgment and field surveys, which were followed by developing a confusion matrix. The confusion matrix plots classified land use practice against the actual land use practice and expresses the overall accuracy as a percentage. The accuracy of the classification found from the confusion matrix is 88% (Table 9.2), which is high. It is important to note that ground truthing points inside the Sundarbans were not included since this is reserved forest and no other land use types will normally be found inside the designated area.

The study found that among the local land use practices, forest (Sundarbans mangrove forest) makes up the largest proportion (36%) of the study area, and 'Gher' covers more area (26%) than agriculture (15%). By utilizing the value coefficients and areas of land use categories (Table 9.1 and 9.2, respectively), the ecosystem service value of land use category 'k', ecosystem services value of southwest coastal Bangladesh can be estimated. The total ecosystem service of the study area was determined as 88 billion US$ (2007 US$). Sundarbans forests alone provide around 84 billion US$, which is around 96% of the total value of ecosystem services. Agriculture and 'gher' land together provide only 1.5% of total ecosystem services. Table 9.3 summarizes the area covered by different land use practices, their contribution towards the total ecosystem services and the coefficient of sensitivity.

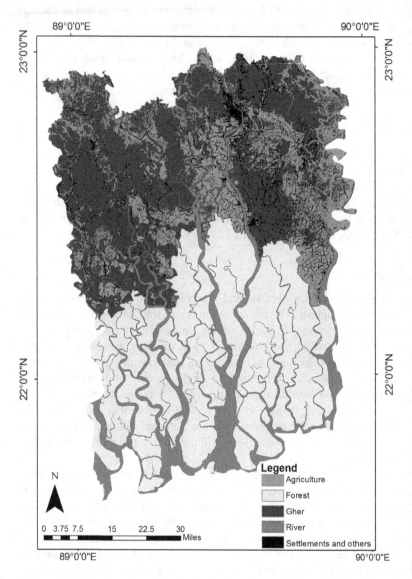

Figure 9.2 Five land use practices in the southwest coastal area of Bangladesh

In all cases, the coefficient of sensitivity was less than unity and often near zero, indicating that the total ecosystem services value estimated in this study area was relatively inelastic with respect to the value coefficients. The coefficient of sensitivity for forest areas was relatively larger because of association between the large area and the high value coefficient. The

Table 9.2 Confusion matrix to determine accuracy of assessment of land use classification

	Agriculture	Gher	River	Settlements and others	Classification overall	Producer accuracy
Agriculture	50	1	9	0	60	88.33%
Gher	5	81	0	3	89	91.01%
River	3	1	27	0	31	87.01%
Settlements and others	0	3	0	17	20	85.00%
Truth over all	58	86	36	20	200	
Overall accuracy	87.50%					

Table 9.3 Land use cover, value of ecosystem service and coefficient of sensitivity

	Land use (ha)	Ecosystem service coefficient ($/ha/year)	Ecosystem service value (billion $)	Percentage contribution %	Coefficient of sensitivity
Agriculture (ha)	185,213	5,567	1.03	1.17	0.01
Forest (ha)	434,377	193,843	84.20	95.42	0.95
Gher (ha)	309,290	614	0.19	0.33	0.01
River (ha)	148,722	12,512	1.86	2.11	0.02
Settlements and other (ha)	128,434	6,661	0.86	0.97	0.01
Total (ha)	1,206,036	–	88.24	100	–

sensitivity analysis indicated that the estimation in this study area was robust despite the value coefficient uncertainties.

Discussion

The method that was used to estimate ecosystem service value in this study was proposed by Costanza *et al.* (1997), deriving ecosystem service value from multiplying the area of land use category and the ecosystem value coefficient. However, as discussed in previous literature, the estimation results by this method are coarse, with deviations and uncertainties due to the complex, dynamic and nonlinear ecosystems (Turner *et al.*, 2003). Land use was used as a proxy measure of ecosystem services. The food production value of wetlands as ecosystem service value to mimic that of 'gher' was an approximation and needs further validation. Moreover, water pollution and soil degradation might cause negative externalities which are not addressed here. Multiplying the area of land use category with an uncertain ecosystem value coefficient will therefore lead to greater uncertainty in total ecosystem service valuation. Different valuation methods may lead to different estimation values, which will necessarily cast doubts on ecosystem service valuation. This study is an effort to estimate the value of ecosystem services at the present time. Sensitivity analysis indicated that the total ecosystem services value estimated in the study area was relatively inelastic with respect to the value coefficients, and the estimate was robust to some extent despite uncertainties in the value coefficients.

Despite some methodological shortcomings, ecosystem service valuation has the potential to inform policy decisions by highlighting the benefits of sustainable ecosystem management (Du *et al.*, 2008). Future studies on ecosystem service valuation in Bangladesh should pay more attention to 'gher' areas, which would help to establish valuations that are more accurate. This will make the techniques of valuation more useful in guiding future human activity towards sustainable land management.

Conclusions

Understanding the value of ecosystem services is of immense importance to initiatives promoting balanced and sustainable use of coastal terrestrial ecosystems, as it underpins the choices about reinstating productive and sustainable food production, balanced against the wider ecological benefits of different types of land use. The ecosystem services value of the southwest coastal area was found to be 88.24 billion US$. The Sundarbans mangrove forest covering 36% of the southwest coastal area provides about 95% of the total ecosystem service (including provisioning (e.g., timber, fuel wood and charcoal), regulating (e.g., flood, storm and erosion control; prevention of salt water intrusion), habitat (e.g., breeding, spawning and nursery habitat for commercial fish species, biodiversity) and cultural services (e.g., recreation, aesthetic, non-use). Since the Sundarbans provides the majority of the total ecosystem services, a small change in the extent of forest cover would have a large impact on total ecosystem service value of this region. Aquaculture is the dominant terrestrial land use of this area now, as agricultural land use covers a smaller area (15%) than 'gher' shrimp ponds (26%). However, agriculture provides five times higher ecosystem services than 'gher'. This is because of the higher ecosystem services (as provisioning services: food, fiber and bioenergy) value provided by agricultural land use compared to 'gher'. Therefore, promoting agriculture could secure more ecosystem services than further developments in 'gher' shrimp production.

Acknowledgements

We express our sincere gratitude to the shrimp farmers and relevant professionals who extended their cooperation during data collection. This work was carried out under the Collaborative Adaptation Research Initiative in Africa and Asia (CARIAA), with financial support from the UK Government's Department for International Development (DFID) and the International Development Research Centre (IDRC), Canada. The views expressed in this work are those of the creators and do not necessarily represent those of DFID and IDRC or its Board of Governors.

References

Akber, M. A., Islam, M. A., Ahmed, M., Rahman, M. M., & Rahman, M. R. (2017). Changes of shrimp farming in southwest coastal Bangladesh. *Aquaculture International, 25*(5), 1883–1899. https://doi.org/10.1007/s10499-017-0159-5

Chen, J., Sun, B., Chen, D., Wu, X., Guo, L. Z., & Wang, G. (2014). Land use changes and their effects on the value of ecosystem services in the small Sanjiang plain in China. *The Scientific World Journal*, 1–17. http://dx.doi.org/10.1155/2014/752846

Costanza, R., D'Arge, R., De Groot, R., Farber, S., Grasso, M., Hannon, B., . . . van den Belt, M. (1997). The value of the world's ecosystem services and natural capital. *Nature, 387*, 253–260. http://dx.doi.org/10.1038/387253a0

Costanza, R., Groot, R. D., Sutton, P., Ploeg, S. V., Anderson, S., Kubiszewski, I., . . . Turner, R. K. (2014). Changes in the global value of ecosystem services. *Global Environmental Change, 26*, 152–158. https://doi.org/10.1016/j.gloenvcha.2014.04.002

Du, H. S., Liu, Z. M., & Zeng, N. (2008). Effects of land use change on ecosystem services value: A case study in the western of Jilin Province. In *Geoinformatics 2008 and Joint Conference on GIS and Built Environment: Monitoring and Assessment of Natural Resources and Environments* (Vol. 7145, p. 71451X). Bellingham, WA: International Society for Optics and Photonics. https://doi.org/10.1117/12.813051

Islam, G. M. T., Islam, A. K. M. S., Shopan, A. A., Rahman, M. M., Lazar, A. N., & Mukhopadhyay, A. (2014). Implications of agricultural land use change to ecosystem services in the Ganges delta. *Journal of Environmental Management, 165*, 443–452. https://doi.org/10.1016/j.jenvman.2014.11.018

Khan, M. M. H., Bryceson, I., Karine, N., Faruque, F., & Rahman, M. M. (2014). Natural disasters and land-use/land-cover change in the Southwest coastal areas of Bangladesh. *Regional Environmental Change, 15*(2), 241–250. https://doi.org/10.1007/s10113-014-0642-8

Konarska, K. M., Sutton, P. C., & Castellon, M. (2002). Evaluating scale dependence of ecosystem service valuation: A comparison of NOAA-AVHRR and Landsat

TM datasets. *Ecological Economics*, *41*(3), 491–507. https://doi.org/10.1016/S0921-8009(02)00096-4

Kreuter, U. P., Harris, H. G., & Matlock, M. D. (2001). Change in ecosystem service values in the San Antonio area, Texas. *Ecological Economics*, *39*(3), 333–346. https://doi.org/10.1016/S0921-8009(01)00250-6

Mendoza-González, G., Martinez, M. L., Lithgow, D., Maqueo, O. P., & Simonin, P. (2014). Land use change and its effects on the value of ecosystem services along the coast of the Gulf of Mexico. *Ecological Economics*, *82*, 23–32. https://doi.org/10.1016/j.ecolecon.2012.07.018

Pandeya, B., Buytaert, W., Zulkafli, Z., Karpouzoglou, T., Mao, F., & Hannah, D. M. (2016). A comparative analysis of ecosystem services valuation approaches for application at the local scale and in data scarce regions. *Ecosystem Services*, *22*, 250–259. https://doi.org/10.1016/j.ecoser.2016.10.015

Tianhong, L., Wenkai, L., & Zhenghan, Q. (2010). Variations in ecosystem service value in response to land use changes in Shenzhen. *Ecological Economics*, *69*(7), 1427–1435. https://doi.org/10.1016/j.ecolecon.2008.05.018

Turner, R. K., Paavola, J., Coopera, P., Farber, S., Jessamya, V., & Georgiou, S. (2003). Valuing nature: Lessons learned and future research directions. *Ecological Economics*, *46*, 493–510. https://doi.org/10.1016/S0921-8009(03)00189-7

Zhao, B., Kreuter, U., Li, B., Ma, Z., Chen, J., & Nakagoshi, N. (2004). An ecosystem service value assessment of land-use change on Chongming Island, China. *Land Use Policy*, *21*(1), 139–148. https://doi.org/10.1016/j.landusepol.2003.10.003

10 Marine Spatial Data Infrastructure for the sustainable management of mangroves in Bangladesh

Opportunities and challenges

Kazi Humayun Kabir, Sharmin Aftab and Shantanu Kumar Saha

Introduction

Located on the northern margin of the Bay of Bengal, the Sundarbans is the largest continuous block of coastal mangrove forest in the world, with some 1,400 km² of outstandingly beautiful wet forest shared between Bangladesh and India. Alongside its status as a World Heritage Site, it is highly productive, supporting not only diverse ecosystems and high levels of biodiversity, but also providing a range of ecosystem services such as barrier protection from coastal sea surges and cyclones, and buffering salt water intrusion into coastal aquifers. It also supports complex human social systems and economic livelihoods based on fishing, shellfish production, tourism, wood and other biological products (Islam & Wahab, 2005; Hasan, 2014; Aziz & Paul, 2015). This entire ecosystem and the rich mixture of unusual and endangered plant and animal species within it (including the Bengal tiger, Ganges and Irrawaddy dolphins, estuarine crocodiles and river terrapins) are threatened by natural and anthropogenic pressures including over-exploitation and illegal forest cutting, changes in coastal cultivation practices, sea port and industrial activities, pollution, reduction in freshwater flows, increased soil and water salinity, natural disasters, climate change and sea level rise (Scialabba, 1998; Roy, 2001; Halpern *et al.*, 2007; Gilman *et al.*, 2008; Miah *et al.*, 2010). Poor planning and management founded on inadequate local knowledge, and growing pressures from tourism over the last 20 years, are adding to the stresses (Rahman *et al.*, 2010).

As a developing country, Bangladesh has for many years faced serious challenges in its search for a sustainable management strategy for the Sunderbans, but recent deliberations on climate change and its potentially negative impacts on mangrove ecosystems have moved policymakers to urgently demand extra protection for the region (Islam & Wahab,

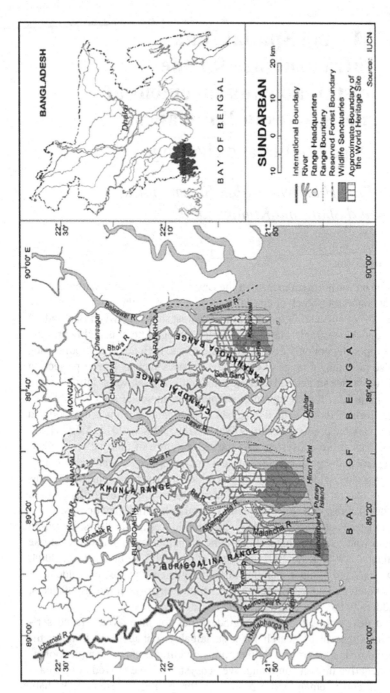

Figure 10.1 Location of the Sundarbans in southwest coastal Bangladesh

Source: International Union for Conservation of Nature [IUCN] (2003) (used with permission)

2005; Shamsuddoha & Chowdhury, 2007). The complexity of the situation makes the managerial requirements almost overwhelming. Truly sustainable development entails mutuality between economic growth, social welfare and environmental protection (Clarke, 2006). When the United Nations Conference on Sustainable Development, or Rio+20, met in Rio de Janeiro in 2012, 20 years on from the original 1992 Earth Summit, it was essential to make progress with a new and more focused development agenda. The political outcome document "The Future We Want" (Bartelmus, 2013) defined clear and practical measures for applying sustainable development principles to the post-2015 development agenda. In September 2015, heads of states and governments agreed on a new generation of 17 Sustainable Development Goals (SDGs), with 169 targets to guide global action until 2030 (Lu *et al.*, 2015). In spite of identifying the significance and necessity, the original outcome document did not explain how reliable geospatial information (i.e., data and technologies) would be combined into the many sustainable development policy and practice processes. Subsequently, the 2030 Agenda for Sustainable Development has provided a new global policy to guide countries' collective management and transformation of the social, economic and environmental dimensions of people and the planet, demanding innovative data acquisition and integration approaches. In theory, this will improve the availability, quality, timeliness and disaggregation of data to support the SDG targets and indicators, but whether this policy provides enough guidelines for countries to implement change and achieve the mandate for the geospatial community to be mainstreamed into sustainable development (Scott & Rajabifard, 2017) remains unanswered.

In Bangladesh as in many tropical countries, a range of organizations is responsible for the sustainable management of mangroves (Iftekhar & Islam, 2004), and they all require decision-support tools to address the multiple issues arising from cross-disciplinary data. Spatial Data Infrastructure (SDI) is the broad term used to summarize the range of concepts, processes, relationships and physical entities for integrated management of spatial information (National Research Council and Mapping Science Committee [NRC and MSC], 1993; McLaughlin & Nichols, 1994; Coleman & McLaughlin, 1998; Infrastructures, 2004; Craglia & Annoni, 2007; Masser & Crompvoets, 2007). Conceptually, it is the process required to integrate technology, policies, criteria, standards and people to promote spatial data use throughout all levels of government. With the aim of improving data access and integration of geospatial information for evidence-based decision and policymaking, SDIs have been developed as a supporting platform that can also be applied to sustainable development challenges (Williamson *et al.*, 2004). Beyond that, in the United States, National SDI (NSDI) was conceived for national-level organizations to "share data" to reduce data production costs and improve spatial data access through networked systems in the country. The problems with "sharing data" have been both technical and institutional, the latter being more challenging (NRC and MSC, 1993). NSDI forms the geospatial platform for wider government strategies and initiatives (Wu *et al.*, 2012) and provides a forum for discussion about enhanced access to high(er) quality geospatial data at lower public cost (Tosta, 1995).

Figure 10.2 sets out NSDI as a national geospatial information system for sustainable development data flow and in many developed countries provides a reliable geospatial data platform enabling connections with other national information systems (Scott & Rajabifard, 2017). An NSDI implementation strategy that is anchored to sustainable development as an overarching theme would provide an "information" approach to national policy in Bangladesh, too.

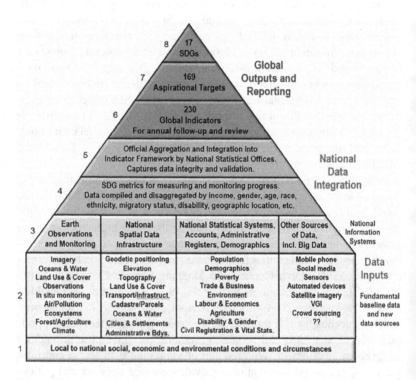

Figure 10.2 A general national information systems of sustainable development "data flow" framework

Source: Scott & Rajabifard (2017) (used with permission)

Research has shown that specific Coastal or Marine Spatial Data Infrastructure (CSDI or MSDI) platforms have been gradually implemented globally since the year 2000 in order to improve the accessibility and the availability of spatial data related to marine and coastal areas (Strain *et al.*, 2006). The term MSDI was first used by the Coast GIS conference series starting in about 1995 to cover the exchange and sharing of marine-themed data (typically including seabed topography, geology, bathymetry, wrecks, offshore installations, pipelines and cables, administrative and legal boundaries, areas of conservation, marine habitats and oceanography) to advance marine and coastal zone administration and management (Vessie *et al.*, 2001). Today it is well accepted that the four basic components of Marine SDI (Strain *et al.*, 2006), namely policy, people and organizations, content and enablers, should be a part of NSDI (Gillespie *et al.*, 2000; Longhorn, 2004; Bartlett *et al.*, 2004).

As Bartlett (2000) points out, given the diversity of interest groups, stakeholders, managerial authorities and administrative structures that converge at the shore, conflicts between and among coastal users, managers, developers and the wider public are almost inevitable, as well as between human society and the natural environment. It is crucial that people and agencies with specific local knowledge and experience of the coastal zone and marine offshore areas and information requirements are an integral part of the NSDI planning process. In this context, the aims to describe the opportunities and challenges are associated with establishing priorities, developing operational definitions and improving integration of MSDI for sustainable management of mangroves in Bangladesh (Stebbins, 2001).

Methodology

The arguments in this chapter are based on an extensive literature search together with 23 key informant interviews (with officials, public actors and social workers, as well as researchers and academics from autonomous, government, non-governmental and private organizations responsible for components and strategies for implementing Marine Spatial Data Infrastructure (MSDI) for sustainable management of the Sundarbans mangroves). Eleven telephone interviews, 12 face-to-face questionnaires (e.g., this organization is involved in developing, supplying or only using spatial data) were carried out in Khulna and Dhaka. For the telephone interviews, telephone numbers of the officials were selected as the heads of their departments from both cities. Telephone surveys were conducted during weekdays office hours (9 a.m.–5 p.m.). All surveys were conducted by the same person (e.g., one of the authors of this paper) from October 2016 to January 2016. Each interview lasted approximately 10–15 minutes. The key questions asked in these interviews were for example: (1) What types of spatial data does your organization produce or use or supply? (2) How could you contribute to developing a National Spatial Data Infrastructure (NSDI) as well as Marine Spatial Data Infrastructure (MSDI)? (3) Is the existing capacity well established for spatial data infrastructure with the ability of sharing interoperable data?

The study also looked at spatial information regarding spatial data production and sharing, and metadata standards for natural and water resource management in the region. The spatial information was needed in order to produce a general information system for a sustainable development data flow among organizations.

Results and discussion

Prospective organizations associate with Marine SDI

Bangladesh, compared to many other countries, has already prioritized the SDGs in its planning policies (Centre for Policy Dialogue [CPD], 2016). With respect to the status of Bangladesh's coastal and marine ecosystems, 14 SDG targets have been finalized by the Government of Bangladesh, relating to *restoring marine and coastal ecosystems*; *science-based management for sustainable marine fisheries*; *significantly reducing land-based marine debris and nutrient pollution*; and *ensuring full access of marine resources to small-scale artisanal fishers*. These capture Bangladesh's urgent need to protect marine resources, along with the policy and strategy formation needed before the main round of work can begin (Arju, 2015). In terms of policy, the Environmental Pollution Control Ordinance (1977) and National Plan of Action (NPoA) already exist to address land-based marine pollution; however, to align more exactly with the demands of the Sustainable Development Goals, the state needs to extend these instruments to address the requirements of survey, monitoring and removal of marine debris, reduction of micro-plastic pollution by consumer products and other industrial wastes and reduction of vessel-based pollution such as ballast water and aquatic species, amongst other priorities. Today's information society, and that of the future, will require integration of the activities of various actors at all levels of the administration into an MSDI that allows accurate and interoperable spatial data capture and storage. For Bangladesh, as for most areas of the world, both public and private organizations are involved in development and management of spatial data related to mangrove and coastal natural resources, and Figure 10.3 shows the integration into a "data cloud" of some of these organizations, with their overlapping jurisdictions; the specific arena for the Marine SDI is shown.

Numerous organizations were identified as being involved in developing spatial data and information in and for the Sundarbans, including government

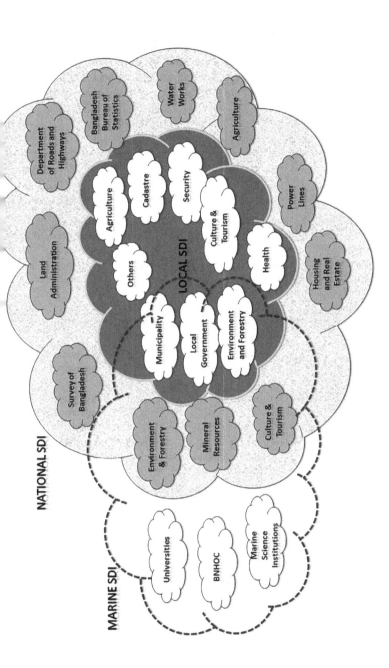

Figure 10.3 Marine Spatial Data Infrastructure (MSDI) is a part of NSDI

Source: Author created

and autonomous, non-government organizations, private organizations and universities having Geographic Information Systems (GIS) installations (Table 10.1). There were 12 state-owned organizations, three NGOs, four private organizations and three universities surveyed who have potentials to be mainstream developers and suppliers of spatial data on the MSDI platform, but the effective range of the different organizations is very wide.

Table 10.1 Major Stakeholders and their role in SDI implementation

Stakeholders	Type of Organization	Numbers of Key Informants Surveyed	Category of user	Datasets
Survey of Bangladesh (SoB)	Autonomous government	1	A, B, C	Topographical maps, geodetic control
Bangladesh Navy Hydrographic and Oceanographic Centre (BNHOC)	Autonomous government	1	A, B, C	Hydrographic and oceanographic data
Bangladesh Geological Survey (BGS)	Autonomous government	1	A, B, C	Geological map
Ministry of Environment and Forest (MoEF)	Government	1	A, B	Fauna and flora, vegetation
Ministry of Fisheries and Livestock	Government	1	A, B	Fish habitat, vegetation and swamp
Ministry of Water Resources	Government	1	A, B, C	water bodies, ocean maps, wetlands
Space Research and Remote Sensing Organizations (SPARRSO)	Autonomous government	1	A, B, C	Satellite images
Ministry of Information and Communication Technology	Government	1	A, C	Geodatabase, spatial objects
Department of Land Record Survey (DLRS)	Autonomous government	1	A, B, C	Land information map
Non-government organizations (NGOs)	NGOs	4	A, C	Socio-economic data
Bangladesh Bureau of Statistics (BBS)	Autonomous government	1	A, B, C	Socio-economic and statistical data

Stakeholders	Type of Organization	Numbers of Key Informants Surveyed	Category of user	Datasets
Private organizations	Private	3		Large-scale data, big data
Department of Forest	Autonomous government	1	C	Forest resource map
Bangladesh Meteorological Department (BMD)	Autonomous government	1	A, B, C	Weather forecasting data
Ministry of Civil Aviation and Tourism	Government	1	A, B, C	Tourism and culture
Universities and other educational institutions	Autonomous and private	3	A, B, C	All kinds of spatial and non-spatial data

A = Producer; B = Supplier; C = User

Bangladesh is typical of developing world nations in that it struggles with the institutional capacity to implement the MSDI. No single agency currently has the entire baseline GIS data for the entire country, or the Sundarbans, which can be shared with all other departments and institutions involved in using geo-spatial information (United Nations Platform for Space-based Information for Disaster Management and Emergency Response [UN-SPIDER], 2014). From Table 10.1, it is clear that most of the organizations are nevertheless engaged in data production activities, duplicating effort in producing and maintaining data-sets that may already be available in another organization. MSDI, appealing as a market, will also have the side effect of creating the cadre of data scientists who are required to assist with other facets of sustainable development; however, the appropriate solution for MSDI will need to be defined by the community itself.

Recent progress with SDI in Bangladesh

An international NSDI conference was held in June 2016, where the Prime Minister of the People's Republic of Bangladesh announced that the govern-ment would ensure the desired development through proper planning, by forming a NSDI to exchange information and data easily among govern-ment, autonomous and non-government institutions. The National Commit-tee on Bangladesh NSDI would provide the necessary guidelines to form the NSDI, and would formulate a law on security of data and information, whilst the Survey of Bangladesh as the National Map Making Institute would be entrusted to form the secretariat. Once the NSDI was formed, various research organizations, teachers and students of various public and private schools, colleges and universities could have uninterrupted access to geospatial information (Rahman, 2016). Consequently, the Survey of Bangladesh now has official responsibility to establish NSDI in consultation with other organizations in Bangladesh. For example, marine and coastal information should preferably be administered by the well-respected Bangladesh Navy Hydrographic and Oceanographic Centre (BNHOC) at Chittagong, with other institutions acting appropriately.

Opportunities and challenges

According to the main stakeholders, the opportunities afforded by MSDI are many, and the main challenges have already been taken into account (Table 10.2); for example, the public appears ready to accept the concept, and transition to securing the required manpower and systems to run the NSDI in Bangladesh is imminent. Wider use of hydrographic data for MSDI could save resources in data acquisition and protect against duplication of efforts. Decision making in coastal management, hazard mapping, fisheries management, oil spill tracking, habitat mapping of sea turtles and other sea animals would all be much easier than before, as reported by specialist staff in the various organizations who were surveyed. Along with these opportunities, MSDI might face hurdles in its implementation phases as a result of an initial lack of skilled manpower, but this problem could easily be overcome in a sustainable manner if there is a political will and coordination.

Table 10.2 Major challenges and opportunities of marine SDI

	Opportunities of MSDI		Challenges of MSDI
1	Wider use of accurate hydrographic data	1	Developing joint policy approaches with other organizations
2	Reduce duplication in data acquisition	2	Investing in initial resources for improved business process/ information management
3	Cost savings, effective use of funds	3	Difficulty in understanding marine SDI components, for the non-marine community
4	Common reference data and metadata	4	Lack of adequate technical, financial and human resources
5	Facilities cooperation amongst information providers	5	Gathering support for SDI activities from decision makers and budget managers
6	Improved decision making such as coastal management, hazard mapping, oil spill tracking and mapping habitats	6	Ensuring correct knowledge, skills and training for staff in different organizations

Conclusion and recommendations

This research concludes that MSDI for Bangladesh is much needed and must be prioritized, in order to address the multidimensional issues of sustainable marine resource management. It has been argued that a common framework and standard of spatial data is required for sustainable management of coastal resources. Challenges such as lack of skilled manpower, political will and difficulties for the non-marine community in understanding MSDI platforms do exist; however, there is a recognition of the benefits of an MSDI platform in managing marine and mangrove resources to support the SDGs. Hence, the government, NGOs, civil society and private organizations need to come forward urgently to take the necessary actions to implement MSDI. They need to work on providing a sound and legal basis that would address the technical and institutional problems of sharing spatial and non-spatial data among a number of institutions. The results drawn from this research reveal that implementation of Bangladesh's MSDI will augment and support Digital Bangladesh initiated by Government of Bangladesh.

References

Arju, M. (2015, October 26). Bangladesh's SDG at the sea. *Daily Sun Bangladesh.* Retrieved from www.daily-sun.com/post/86162/Bangladesh%E2%80%99s-SDG-at-the-Sea

Aziz, A., & Paul, A. R. (2015). Bangladesh Sundarbans: Present status of the environment and biota. *Diversity, 7*(3), 242–269.

Bartelmus, P. (2013). The future we want: Green growth or sustainable development? *Environmental Development, 7,* 165–170.

Bartlett, D. J. (2000). Working on the Frontiers of Science: Applying GIS to the Coastal Zone. In D. J. Wright, & D. J. Barlett (Eds.), *Marine and Coastal Geographical Information Systems* (pp. 11–24). London: Taylor & Francis.

Bartlett, D. J., Longhorn, R., & Garriga, M. (2004, February). *Marine and Coastal Data Infrastructures: A Missing Piece in the SDI Puzzle.* 7th Global Spatial Data Infrastructure Conference, Bangalore, India.

Centre for Policy Dialogue. (2016). *Citizen's Platform Brief.* Bangladesh: Citizen's Platform for SDGs and Dhaka, Bangladesh: Center for Policy Dialogue.

Clarke, A. C. (2006). Towards a future maritime policy for the Union: A European vision for the oceans and seas: Part two. *RevistadelInstituto de Navegación de España: publicacióntécnicacuatrimestral de navegaciónmarítima, aérea, espacial y terrestre, 27,* 46.

Coleman, D. J., & McLaughlin, J. D. (1998). Defining global geospatial data infrastructure (GGDI): Components, stakeholders and interfaces. *Geomatica-Ottawa, 52,* 129–143.

Craglia, M., & Annoni, A. (2007). Inspire: An innovative approach to the development of spatial data infrastructures in Europe. *Research and Theory in Advancing Spatial Data Infrastructure Concepts, 93–105.*

Gillespie, R., Butler, M., Anderson, N., Kucera, H., & LeBlanc, C. (2000). MGDI: An information infrastructure to support integrated coastal management in Canada. *GeoCoast*, *1*(1), 15–24.

Gilman, E. L., Ellison, J., Duke, N. C., & Field, C. (2008). Threats to mangroves from climate change and adaptation options: A review. *Aquatic Botany*, *89*(2), 237–250.

Halpern, B. S., Selkoe, K. A., Micheli, F., & Kappel, C. V. (2007). Evaluating and ranking the vulnerability of global marine ecosystems to anthropogenic threats. *Conservation Biology*, *21*(5), 1301–1315.

Hasan, M. (2014). *Features of Forestry in Bangladesh and Available Legal Protections and Implications*. Dhaka, Bangladesh: Bepress, University of Dhaka.

Iftekhar, M. S., & Islam, M. R. (2004). Managing mangroves in Bangladesh: A strategy analysis. *Journal of Coastal Conservation*, *10*(1), 139–146.

Infrastructures, D. S. D. (2004). *The SDI Cookbook*. GSDI/Nebert.

International Union for Conservation of Nature. (2003). *Status of the Ecological Integrity of the Sundarbans*. IUCN Bangladesh Country Office.

Islam, M. S., & Wahab, M. A. (2005). A review on the present status and management of mangrove wetland habitat resources in Bangladesh with emphasis on mangrove fisheries and aquaculture. In H. Segers & K. Martens (Eds.), *Aquatic Biodiversity II* (pp. 165–190). Dordrecht: Springer.

Longhorn, R. A. (2004). Coastal spatial data infrastructure. In D. Bartlett, & J. Smith (Eds.), *GIS for Coastal Zone Management* (pp. 1–15). Boca Raton, FL: CRC Press, Taylor & Francis.

Lu, Y., Nakicenovic, N., Visbeck, M., & Stevance, A. S. (2015). Five priorities for the UN sustainable development goals. *Nature*, *520*(7548), 432–433.

Masser, I., & Crompvoets, J. (2007). *Building European Spatial Data Infrastructures* (Vol. 380). Redlands, CA: Esri Press.

McLaughlin, J., & Nichols, S. (1994). Developing a national spatial data infrastructure. *Journal of Surveying Engineering*, *120*(2), 62–76.

Miah, G., Bari, N., & Rahman, A. (2010). Resource degradation and livelihood in the coastal region of Bangladesh. *Frontiers of Earth Science in China*, *4*(4), 427–437.

National Research Council, & Mapping Science Committee. (1993). *Toward a Coordinated Spatial Data Infrastructure for the Nation*. Washington D.C, USA: National Academies Press.

Rahman, M. M., Rahman, M. M., & Islam, K. S. (2010). The causes of deterioration of Sundarban mangrove forest ecosystem of Bangladesh: Conservation and sustainable management issues. *Aquaculture, Aquarium, Conservation & Legislation-International Journal of the Bioflux Society (AACL Bioflux)*, *3*(2).

Rahman, S. M. (2016, June 1). *Spatial Data Infrastructure for Country's Planned Progress: PM*. The Independent Bangladesh. Retrieved from www.theindependbd.com/post/45829

Roy, P. K. (2001). *Coastal Resource Degradation and User-Right Abuse in Bangladesh: An Overview of the Challenges in User-Based Community Management*. Proceedings from Forging Unity: Coastal Communities and the Indian Ocean's Future, 160–171. Chennai, India. Retrieved from http://aquaticcommons.org/3387/1/ALL%2827%29.pdf

Scialabba, N. (Ed.). (1998). *Integrated Coastal Area Management and Agriculture, Forestry and Fisheries.* Rome, Italy: Food & Agriculture Organization. Retrieved from http://www.fao.org/docrep/W8440e/W8440e00.htm

Scott, G., & Rajabifard, A. (2017). Sustainable development and geospatial information: A strategic framework for integrating a global policy agenda into national geospatial capabilities. *Geo-Spatial Information Science, 20*(2), 59–76.

Shamsuddoha, M., & Chowdhury, R. K. (2007). *Climate Change Impact and Disaster Vulnerabilities in the Coastal Areas of Bangladesh.* COAST Trust, Dhaka.

Stebbins, R. A. (2001). *Exploratory Research in the Social Sciences* (Vol. 48). Thousand Oaks, CA: SAGE. doi: 10.4135/9781412984249

Strain, L., Rajabifard, A., & Williamson, I. (2006). Marine administration and spatial data infrastructure. *Marine Policy, 30*(4), 431–441.

Tosta, N. (1995). *Data Policies and the National Spatial Data Infrastructure.* Proceedings of the Conference on Law and Information Policy for Spatial Databases. NCGIA, University of Maine, Orono.

United Nations Platform for Space-Based Information for Disaster Management and Emergency Response. (2014). *UN-SPIDER Brochure 2014.* Vienna, Austria: United Nations.

Vessie, D., van de Poll, R., Nichols, S., & Monahan, D. (2001). *GIS Mapping and Analysis Tools for Use within the Coastal Zone.* Coastal GeoTools'01: Proceedings of the 2nd Biennial Coastal GeoTools Conference[np]. Charleston, SC, January 8–11, 2001.

Williamson, I. P., Rajabifard, A., & Feeney, M. E. F. (Eds.). (2004). *Developing Spatial Data Infrastructures: From Concept to Reality.* London and New York: CRC Press, Taylor & Francis.

Wu, D., Georgiadou, P. Y., Kapur Keeble, O., Bennett, R. M., Brussel, M. J. G., Lance, K. T., . . . van Westen, C. J. (2012). *Geospatial Science and technology for development: With a focus on urban development, land administration and disaster risk management.* (UNCTAD Current Studies on Science, Technology and Innovation; No. 6). Geneva: United Nations Conference on Trade and Development (UNCTAD).

Index

Note: Figures and tables are denoted with italicized and bold page numbers, respectively; end note information is denoted with an n and note number following the page number.

Printed in the United States
by Baker & Taylor Publisher Services